The Light and the Glory for Children reveals to youngsters ages 9–12 how God's loving, guiding, and protecting hand has been upon our country from the very beginning. Both your children and you will enjoy following the exciting story of the birth and early growth of "one nation under God"—from Christopher Columbus's voyage in 1492 to George Washington's inauguration in 1783. They will witness the joys and triumphs of those who remained faithful to God and the sad outcome for those who compromised their faith for wealth and power in the New World.

With conversations that bring people and events to life, questions for discussion, and a glossary, this book is both fun and informative. *The Light and the Glory for Children* shows how God intervened time and again in the events of early American history to accomplish His grand plan for a very special place where His followers could worship freely.

Just as your children will enjoy *The Light and the Glory for Children*, you're sure to appreciate these enlightening best-sellers that show the part God played in America's past and compel us to consider His plan for the country's future:

The Light and the Glory

Peter Marshall and David Manuel trace God's plan for America from the fruition of Columbus's dream to Washington's inauguration. In this dynamic, enlightening volume, the authors challenge Americans to return to God and rediscover the destiny that was ours from the beginning.

From Sea to Shining Sea

Peter Marshall and David Manuel present a powerful sequel that chronicles God's intervention in American history from Washington's presidency to the brink of the Civil War.

The
LIGHT
and the
GLORY
For Children

*Discovering God's Plan
for America from
Christopher Columbus
to George Washington*

Peter Marshall
&
David Manuel

with
Anna Wilson Fishel

Fleming H. Revell
A Division of Baker Book House Co
Grand Rapids, Michigan 49516

THE LIGHT AND THE GLORY FOR CHILDREN

The material in this book has been carefully researched and is historically accurate, but specific scenes and conversations have been fictionalized to heighten the drama and foster its readability.

Scripture quotations are from the New American Standard Bible, © The Lockman Foundation, 1960, 1962, 1963, 1968, 1971, 1972, 1973, 1975, 1977.

Library of Congress Cataloging-in-Publication Data

Marshall, Peter
    The light and the glory for children / Peter Marshall and David Manuel, with Anna Wilson Fishel.
    p. cm.
    Summary: Uses a Christian perspective to examine the history of America from the first voyage of Columbus to the aftermath of the Revolutionary War, with an emphasis on faithfulness to God's Word.
    ISBN 0-8007-5448-4
    1. United States–History–Colonial period, ca. 1600-1775–Juvenile literature. 2. United States–History–Revolution, 1775-1783–Juvenile literature. 3. United States–Church history–Colonial period, ca. 1600-1775–Juvenile literature. 4. History (Theology)–Juvenile literature. 5. Providence and government of God–Juvenile literature. [1. United States–History. 2. Christian life.] I. Manuel, David. II. Fishel, Anna Wilson, III. Title.
E189.M3615 1992
973–dc20

                                                 92-11727
                                                  CIP
                                                  AC

Book development by March Media, Inc.

Copyright © 1992 by Peter Marshall and David Manuel
Published by Fleming H. Revell
a division of Baker Book House Company
P.O. Box 6287, Grand Rapids, Michigan 49516-6287
www.revellbooks.com

ISBN: 0-8007-5448-4

Seventeenth printing, August 2004

Printed in the United States of America

CONTENTS

RELIVING
THE ADVENTURE

The ability to imagine is a wonderful gift from God; before television, it was how everyone relived the adventures of the real-life heroes of history. It can still be done, whenever you read a book.

In this book, you can stand on the deck of the *Santa Maria* alongside Christopher Columbus, sailing farther and farther westward, going boldly where no man had ever gone before. . . .

A century (and a few pages) later, you can journey with the great explorer-missionaries who opened vast reaches of the Southwest and the wilderness north of the Great Lakes. With Father Jacques Marquette, you can paddle down the mighty river that divides this continent, the one the native Americans called the Mississippi. . . .

You can join the Pilgrims, as they start their little colony in Plymouth and celebrate the first Thanksgiving in the New World, with the Wampanoag tribe. . . .

From the colony of Georgia to the colony of Massachusetts, you can ride on horseback with George Whitefield, the first evangelist to come to America. As he preaches, you can see whole towns become excited about living for God. . . .

You can share the growing concern of the colonists, as King George of England taxes them unfairly and punishes them if they object. And you can decide if you would have remained loyal to England or joined the patriots in their struggle to keep the freedom that their ancestors had known for 150 years. . . .

In July 1776, you can be present in Philadelphia for the great debate which resulted in America's Declaration of Independence. . . .

On Brooklyn Heights, you can wait in the trenches with the other Patriots, surrounded and outnumbered by the British—and then see the extraordinary fog that came and stayed, enabling you and the entire American army to escape to Manhattan. Both sides called that fog a miracle. . . .

In the cold winter of 1777-78, in Valley Forge, you can discover General Washington, alone and kneeling in the snow, praying. . . .

And you can be by his side at Yorktown, when he wins the victory that guarantees the United States of America will survive. . . .

You can return to Philadelphia's Independence Hall in 1787, where once again the future of our country is at stake. Now the new States' delegates are trying to agree on the form our government will take. But no one can agree on anything, until Benjamin Franklin gets to his feet. He reminds them that when they were up against the mightiest military power on earth, the only thing that saved them was prayer. . . .

This book is full of heroes—real men and women who

were not afraid to share their faith and let it guide them in all the things they did. It made the difference in their personal lives—just as it can in yours.

Let their example inspire you to make sure our nation stays on course!

Peter Marshall
David Manuel

I am well aware of the toil and blood and treasure that it will cost us to maintain this Declaration, and support and defend these States. Yet through all the gloom I can see rays of ravishing light and glory. I can see that the end is worth more than all the means.

–John Adams to Abigail Adams
on the passing of
the Declaration of Independence

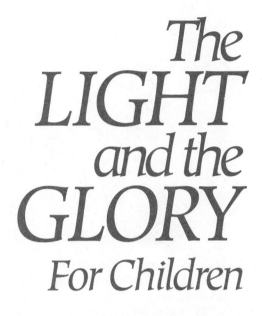

The
LIGHT
and the
GLORY
For Children

1. 1492 — Columbus discovers America.
2. 1607 — Powhatan helps the settlers at Jamestown.
3. 1673 — Marquette and Joliet come down the Mississippi River to Illinois.
4. 1630 — The Puritans live the Covenant Way in New England.
5. 1736 — George Whitefield begins preaching in the colonies.
6. 1773 — The Colonists revolt against the British tax on tea.
7. 1775 — Paul Revere warns the Colonists that the British troops are coming.
8. 1789 — George Washington takes the oath of office as the first president of the United States.

CHAPTER ONE

*The Lord called me from the womb. From the body
of my mother He named Me. . . . I will make You a
light of the nations so that My salvation may reach
to the end of the earth. (Isaiah 49:1, 6)*

CHRIST-BEARER

 In the year 1271, an Italian explorer named Marco Polo set out on a long and dangerous journey across land and sea. He traveled to the Indies, which were the countries of India, China, and Japan. When he returned to Europe, Polo carried back many treasures such as spices, ivory, and silk.

The Europeans liked these things and wanted more of them. So they began to look for different trade routes to the Indies. But land travel from Europe to the Far East was long and treacherous. The only known sea route at that time was around the continent of Africa.

Christopher Columbus was the first European to sail west through the waters of the Atlantic Ocean. He discovered the continents of North and South America. Many historians believe that he was simply looking for a better trade route. They think his discovery was an accident. But was it? What really lay behind his desire to sail west?

As you will see, it was something very great. It was the plan of God Almighty.

✝ ✝ ✝

Christopher Columbus grew up in the seaport town of Genoa, Italy, where his father owned a wool shop. In 1484, he moved to Lisbon, Portugal, to work with his brother Bartolomeo, who made maps for shipowners. At that time, Lisbon was the seafaring capital of the world. Many ships came and went from its ports. The Portuguese were great explorers. They already knew the earth was round. If only they could find a better way to get to the Indies.

A God-given love of the sea took Christopher out on the ocean many times. He learned how to plot the course of a ship and how to locate its position. This is called navigation. He gathered the newest geographical information. He studied the latest maps, and he began to think about a voyage of his own.

Columbus kept a journal. In it he wrote that God Himself had given him the idea to sail west into the Atlantic Ocean. "It was the Lord who put into my mind the fact that it would be possible to sail from here to the Indies," he explained. "There is no question that the inspiration was from the Holy Spirit."

Columbus sensed God's leading. He could cross the Atlantic and discover another trade route. But he could do something more. He could undertake this in the name of Jesus and carry the Gospel message to distant lands. Columbus was going to be a missionary explorer and spread the Good News about Jesus.

The young sailor marked charts and plotted the course. Yes, it could be done. Now he had to find a country that would give him enough money to carry out the mission.

Columbus first presented his plan to the king of Portugal. He also sent his brother to talk with King Henry of England. Neither king liked the idea, and both turned him down. So Columbus approached the country of Spain.

Columbus waited over four years for King Ferdinand and Queen Isabella of Spain to give him an answer. They said *no*. It was 1490, and Spain was at war with the Moors. The country could not afford such an expedition. The king and queen told Columbus to come back after the war.

That day Columbus left the court to return to La Rábida. La Rábida was the monastery in which he was staying. Columbus walked slowly down the road. He felt sad and lonely. Doubts filled his mind.

"Where did I go wrong?" he mumbled to himself. His eyes filled with tears. With a sigh, he placed his hands in the pockets of his pantaloons.

"Maybe I've been wrong from the start," he mumbled. "Maybe this is not God's vision after all. Maybe everyone is right—it's not a good idea."

Inside La Rábida lived an old monk named Juan Peréz. He was a man of great spiritual wisdom. That night Columbus talked with Juan Peréz. The monk listened carefully. Columbus shared his belief that God Almighty was telling him to carry the message of Christ across the Atlantic. The two men prayed.

That night at La Rábida marked a turning point in the story of Columbus. The monk was a friend of Queen Isabella. The next morning Peréz wrote to her that God's hand was upon Columbus. He asked her to consider the proposal again.

And she did. She sent word for Columbus to meet the royal court in the city of Santa Fé.

In Santa Fé, Spain was celebrating a huge victory over the Moors. By the time Columbus reached the city, the Spanish monarchs were ready to accept his idea. They wanted a way to thank God for their victory over the Moors. And Columbus offered them the way. He would be one of Spain's ambassadors to distant lands. The king and queen agreed to his plan and would pay for the voyage.

Columbus had waited years for this moment! He stood straight and tall as the king spoke to him. But as he listened, his heart began to swell. He began to think about the riches and honor which would be his when he discovered these places.

"Your Majesty," Columbus began, "I must thank you for this honor and for your faith in me. But I must request something else."

"What is it?" King Ferdinand asked.

Pride filled the sailor's voice. He spoke boldly.

"When I discover these lands," Columbus said, "I want to be governor over them. I also want one-tenth of all the riches I find. And I want you to make me an admiral."

The king and queen stared at Columbus.

"This is too much!" the king replied angrily. "You're dismissed at once!"

Columbus had let his sinful nature take control by asking for power and riches. And he almost lost his golden opportunity, but God was watching over him. A friend named Luis de Santangel later persuaded the king and queen to accept the proposal. Spain would finance the expedition after all.

✛ ✛ ✛

Eight months later, the *Niña, Pinta,* and *Santa Maria* set sail "in the name of Jesus." It was August 3, 1492.

A tall, red-haired man stood on the deck of the *Santa Maria*. His clear, blue eyes looked out at the great ocean around him. His rugged, brown face showed a man who had known many years of life on the high seas. As the ship rolled with the waves, Columbus held the rail with steady hands. He shouted commands to the sailors and watched them obey.

The date was October 9, 1492. Three small Spanish ships called caravels sailed along in a calm sea. Martin Pinzón and his brother, Vincent, were captains of the *Pinta* and the *Niña*. They had come to the *Santa Maria* for an emergency meeting with the commander, Columbus. As the Pinzón brothers climbed aboard the *Santa Maria*, tension filled the air.

Columbus welcomed the two captains into his private cabin. His smile disappeared when he saw their expressions. They did not look happy.

"Commander, things are not going well," Martin Pinzón began. "Our men are tired. They are scared and grumbling. We have not seen land for thirty-one days. You do not even know if there is land ahead."

"We are too far away from Spain, sir," Vincent continued. "And we don't know what lies ahead. You must turn the ships around."

Columbus sighed. Was there anything except water ahead of them?

Silently, Columbus walked over to the window of his cabin. He gazed out at the golden sun as it set below the sparkling sea in front of them. The Pinzóns wanted him to cancel the voyage. They were asking him to give up all his hopes and dreams. This voyage was his mission in life. How could he quit now? He had waited eight long years to set sail. He had been rejected and called a fool. If he turned back now, everyone in Europe would laugh at him. He would not get another chance.

The Pinzón brothers were waiting for his answer. Should he stop the mission and turn back? The commander turned to face his two captains.

"I know we've been sailing for a long time," he began. "We've been heading due west from the Canary Islands for thirty-one days. I realize the men can't take much more. I've heard their talk." Columbus stopped and swallowed hard

"You're right," he whispered. "We'll turn back."

With a heavy heart, Columbus glanced out the porthole again.

"But you must give me one thing," he continued. "I want three more days on this course. Just three days. Tell the men that if we don't sight land by October 12, we will head home."

The Pinzón brothers agreed and returned to their ships. Columbus remained alone in his cabin. He could hear the groaning masts of the *Santa Maria*. He could feel her steady movement through the smooth waters. How he loved the ocean! How he had dreamed about this voyage. But that did not seem to matter anymore. It was all over now. Columbus collapsed at his desk and began to scribble on the paper. He wrote his name, Christopher . . . *Christo-ferens*. In Latin his name meant "Christ-bearer."

What would happen over the next three days? To turn back meant defeat. Columbus felt defeated. Yet God was still God, and He always answered prayers. Humbly, the commander knelt in his cabin and prayed.

Over the next three days, amazing things happened. At first, the three ships began to speed through the water. In fact, they flew so fast that the sailors grew frightened because they were sailing even farther from home! Then on the second day, men on the *Pinta* saw a reed and a small piece of carved wood floating in the water. These were definite signs of land. Everyone grew excited.

At ten o'clock that night, Columbus and one of his sailors thought they spotted a tiny light far in the distance. Columbus took this as encouragement from the Lord. The ships pressed on.

Then at two o'clock in the morning, the lookout aboard the *Pinta* sighted a low, white cliff shining in the moonlight. "Land! Land!" he cried.

⌐The *Pinta* fired its cannon to signal the others. With just four hours left until the dawn of the third day, they had discovered land! It was October 12, 1492.⌐

Immediately, the three caravels turned south to avoid hitting the reefs near shore. They sailed until daybreak. As the sun rose, they reached the southern tip of the island. The coastline began to glow in the morning sun. The sailors gazed across the clear, blue water to the shore. Silently, they stood on the decks of their ships. They knew this day was important. They had discovered an unknown land three thousand miles from home. It was a day no one would forget.

At noon, the landing party rowed ashore. Every officer had dressed in his best uniform. Columbus carried the Spanish flag. As the men waded toward shore, they addressed Columbus by the new title: "Admiral of the Ocean Sea." Their eyes filled with tears when they reached the beach. The sailors knelt in the sand and bowed their heads. The admiral prayed. He named the island *San Salvador*, which meant "Holy Savior." He and his men erected a huge cross on the beach in honor of the Savior. And then he thanked God for using them to proclaim His Holy Name in this second part of the earth.

Short, dark-skinned people welcomed the explorers to San Salvador. These people believed the Spaniards were friendly white gods who had come down from heaven in canoes pulled by white clouds. They had never seen white men or sailing ships. Columbus called the natives "Indians" because he thought he had landed on an island in the Indies.

The Spaniards offered the Indians gifts of red hats and glass beads. Columbus wanted to treat them kindly, and he wanted to tell them about Jesus.

Since the natives did not speak Spanish, they used a type of sign language with the sailors. Columbus questioned them about the tiny gold ornaments worn around their necks. The Indians told him about the gold located south of San Salvador. The Spaniards got excited and decided to sail southwest in search of gold.

The three caravels set sail, stopping at many islands and putting up crosses for the Lord Jesus. However, they did not find gold. When the *Pinta* turned off toward the island of Babeque, the *Niña* and the *Santa Maria* tried to follow. Bad weather forced the two vessels to another island. They named this one *Española*. And here, Columbus experienced a sea captain's nightmare.

It was dawn on Christmas morning. The *Santa Maria* floated calmly in a cove off the island. Everyone was asleep except a young ship's boy, who guarded the ship's tiller. The boy did not notice the waves gently moving the ship toward shore. Suddenly the rudder under the ship became stuck. The boy cried out. Admiral Columbus ran topside to see what had happened. The *Santa Maria* had struck a reef! Disaster!

"Get to the anchor!" Columbus yelled. "We might be able to free the rudder before the tide goes out!"

The men hurried, but it was too late. The *Santa Maria* was stuck. As the tide went out, sharp rocks appeared and cut into the bottom of the ship. Water poured into her hull. The damaged vessel leaned over in the water. She would never sail again.

Friendly natives from the island helped the seamen unload the ship's cargo. On Española the Spaniards found gold at last. And here, the admiral also set up the first settlement in the New World. He called it *La Navidad*, which means "the Nativity." Thirty-nine men remained on Española as the first settlers.

Columbus boarded the *Niña*. It was time to return to Spain. The little caravel began to weave its way back through the islands. Three days out, she met the *Pinta*. The two ships sailed together into calm seas and sunny skies.

A steady wind pushed them through the waters of the Atlantic. For much of the voyage, the men thanked God for the good weather. And then came the storm.

On the night of February 12, 1493, the *Niña* and the *Pinta* sailed into a huge storm. Great waves crashed down on the decks, tossing the ships to and fro. The winds howled. Heavy rains pounded the men as they labored against the waves. On the first night, the two little ships lost sight of each other.

Why? Columbus agonized as he prayed in his cabin. *Why is this happening, Lord? Do You want us to sink? Don't You want us to return to Spain with the good news about our discovery?*

CHAPTER TWO

If you return to the Almighty, you will be restored.
(Job 22:23)

IF GOLD IS YOUR ALMIGHTY

Christopher Columbus had sailed across the Atlantic Ocean and discovered a great, unknown land. God had given him a vision, and he had carried it out. But just as he was almost back to Spain, he had to battle this terrible storm. Columbus knew God must have a reason. But what was it?

The answer lay deep within the man's own heart. God saw that the sailor was becoming very proud. Columbus deserved to be called admiral. He had discovered a new land and a new people. Soon the admiral would become rich and famous. God was concerned that he would let those things take priority in his life. He was concerned that Columbus would forget his true mission. God wanted Columbus to return to Spain in obedience and humility to Him. Such a bad storm should have warned Columbus to search his own heart and seek forgiveness.

Would Columbus hear God's message? Would he return to Spain relying on the Almighty? Or would riches and power become his gods?

✟   ✟   ✟

The storm raged on for nearly a week. When at last it came to an end, Columbus and the sailors sighed with relief.

And then, toward evening, a blessed sight appeared. Far away on the northeast horizon lay the Azores, a group of tiny islands off the coast of Portugal. The explorers had made it home. The date was Tuesday, February 19, 1493. Columbus and his men stopped to rest.

When the *Niña* set out again, she ran into another storm. The little ship once again battled fierce winds and rain. This time she lost her sails. For five days the storm propelled the ship through the water. Then on the sixth day, the crew spotted land. It was the coast of Portugal.

By now, the winds were blowing the ship straight toward the rocky coast. Admiral Columbus knew they had one chance. If he could steer the vessel into the nearby River of Lisbon, they would be safe. This meant he had to turn the ship broadside into the wind. And this was dangerous because she could turn over. God would have to be with them.

The admiral wiped the rain from his eyes. Could he do it?

"Lean her to starboard!" Columbus yelled to the helmsman. "Keep her to the right. Yes, that's it. Now hold her there—steady, steady as she goes."

The *Niña* slowly turned toward the coast. But the wind and waves kept pushing her closer and closer to the rocks.

"Hold her now," Columbus shouted. "Don't let go! We have to make it into the river."

All at once, water came crashing over the ship's starboard side.

"She's tipping over!" the helmsman yelled.

"We're going to drown!" another sailor screamed.

The nervous admiral held his breath. Then, slowly but surely, the little vessel righted herself in the water! The crew worked harder. The *Niña* straightened up as the storm howled. Finally, a large wave pushed her directly into the mouth of the Lisbon River. It was a miracle. They had made it. The sailors clapped and danced with joy. Columbus sighed with relief—God had been with them.

Because of the weather, Columbus visited King John of Portugal for a while. He did not stay long, though. He wanted to get home.

[On March 15, 1493, Columbus and his sailors finally entered the harbor of Palos, Spain.]Good news awaited them. The *Pinta* had not been lost. She had been blown to the coast of Africa, and she was now on her way home. It was time for a great celebration.

Columbus traveled to Barcelona, which was the winter home of King Ferdinand and Queen Isabella. The city was prepared for him. Colorful flags decorated the streets. Spanish capes hung on the sides of the buildings. Women threw rose petals from the balcony windows. People crowded the streets.

Columbus led the small procession on horseback. His officers, some cargo wagons, and six Indian natives followed him. The admiral sat tall and erect in his saddle. One hand held the reins. The other rested proudly on his hip. As the parade reached the palace, the crowd cheered. Columbus waved.

That evening, Columbus and his group entered the grand throne room. Hundreds of candles brightened the court with its great marble columns. As Columbus approached the throne, the monarchs stood up to greet him. Columbus knelt to kiss their hands, but they made him stand. Then they ordered a special chair to be brought for him. The crowd was amazed.

King Ferdinand began, "We are most anxious to hear about your voyage, Commander."

The court listened as Columbus related his story. He told about the long journey across the Atlantic. He described San Salvador and the kind natives. He told them about Española and losing the *Santa Maria*. He introduced them to the Indians who had sailed back with him. They walked forward wearing their native clothes and carrying native wildlife. The king and queen had never seen such strange animals as jungle rats, parrots, and dogs that could not bark.

Columbus next motioned his officers to pick up the oak chest. The officers carried it to him. Columbus stood and walked toward the chest.

"Your Majesties," he announced, "it is with great pleasure that I present this to you and to Spain."

Columbus threw open the lid. Everyone's eyes opened wide. The chest was filled with gold! There were masks and crowns of pure gold, and bright gold jewelry shone in the candlelight. The chest even held gold nuggets. Anyone who had doubted Columbus before did not doubt now. He had made a great discovery—the Indies had gold!

King Ferdinand and Queen Isabella stared at the contents of the oak chest. They both stood and then fell to their knees, lifting their faces toward heaven. In the throne room of Spain that night, everyone gave thanks to Almighty God.

Columbus was a hero. He had kept his promise to Spain by discovering a new land, a new people, and great riches. Now Spain would keep her promise to him. The king and queen officially titled Columbus "Admiral of the Ocean Sea." They pronounced him governor of the new land. And they gave him permission to receive one-tenth of all the riches.

Columbus had kept his promise to God, but something was changing deep within his heart. In appreciation for what he did, Spain gave the admiral 335,000 maravedis. This was a lot of money, but it was not enough for Columbus. He wanted more. He demanded that 10,000 maravedis be paid annually to the first person to sight land. The lookout aboard the *Pinta* had spotted land first, but Columbus took the prize. The Admiral was letting gold become his god.

The first voyage to the New World had been a success. On the second voyage across the Atlantic in 1493, seventeen ships and twelve hundred men accompanied Columbus. They dreamed of gold and adventure, but their dreams soon turned into nightmares.

When the ships arrived at the settlement of La Navidad, none of the settlers were there. The natives had killed all thirty-nine men. Columbus quickly found out what happened.

Soon after the *Niña* had sailed for Spain the year before, the settlers had started hurting the native women and stealing the Indians' gold. The natives could not stop them. At last, the angry Indians ambushed the men, killing every one of them.

As governor of Española, Columbus had a big problem. His men now hated the natives for what they had done to the

Spanish settlers. His men also did not trust him anymore. They no longer believed his stories of gentle natives and abundant gold. Columbus had lost their respect and his authority. How could he control them now?

The governor knew he had to do something, and he had to do it fast. But he did not think to get on his knees and pray. He did not think to ask His Heavenly Father to forgive him for his greed and selfishness. He tried to work things out by himself.

Gold, he thought to himself. *I'll start exploring for gold. That will make the men forget what has happened here.*

So Columbus had the men search the island for gold. But everything went wrong. Disease-bearing mosquitoes plagued them. The heat spoiled their food. Many of the men became sick with terrible fevers. And no one found any gold.

Columbus *had* to come up with some gold, so he made the Indians pay a tax in gold. If they could not pay, the Spanish punished them and treated them like slaves. In just four years, most of the native population had died or been killed. It was a massacre.

The governor decided to return home. In Spain, he learned that the king and queen were very concerned about the Indians.

"Governor Columbus," King Ferdinand began, "you must understand. We are responsible to God for the welfare of our people. And now these natives are our people. This terrible treatment cannot continue. You must govern the Indians as we would govern them."

Columbus sighed. He knew the king was right.

The king continued, "We must also discuss the gold. It's

true that we want you to find gold because it would help our country. But we don't want such riches at the expense of the Indians! Now see to it that our desires are carried out!"

The king and queen knew they had to be firm with Columbus. He was a good explorer, but he was not proving to be a very good governor. He was proud and demanding. He spoke harshly and got mad easily. The people in the islands did not respect him. And he refused to take responsibility for what was happening. Yet, the monarchs let him return as soon as a small fleet of ships was ready.

After a long and terrible journey, the Spanish ships reached Española. Columbus discovered that rebellion had broken out among the men he had left on his earlier voyage. The inhabitants no longer wanted him to be governor. He had lost his authority over them, and he could not control the situation. Alarming reports went back to the king and queen.

The Spanish monarchs had no choice but to replace Columbus as governor. They dispatched Francisco de Bobadilla, who carried a letter giving him authority to act as governor. When the new governor's caravel arrived in Española, he discovered seven Spanish bodies dangling on ropes. Then he learned that five more were to be hanged the next morning. Immediately, Bobadilla installed himself as governor. But Columbus refused to honor the proclamation from the king and queen.

"I am governor of these islands," he informed Bobadilla. "This is my land. I discovered it. The king and queen have no right to take away my authority!"

"Put this man in chains!" Bobadilla ordered. "I am sending him back to Spain for trial."

Columbus remained in chains until he reported to the king and queen in December 1500. They were shocked and ordered the chains removed. But they did not appoint him governor again. Columbus begged them to send him back to the New World. A year later, they permitted him to go, but only to explore for gold.

Once again, Columbus was looking for gold. It had become the most important thing in his life. In Columbus's heart, God now held second place.

Despite the king and queen's command that he not sail to Española, Columbus sailed directly for the island. The governor refused to let him enter, so he sailed to Cuba. Then he sailed southeast toward Central America. The trip usually took three or four days, but strong headwinds stretched the trip into thirty-nine days! God Himself seemed to be blocking the voyage. Yet Columbus never considered he might not be doing God's will.

The four caravels proceeded down the coasts of what are now Honduras, Nicaragua, and Costa Rica in Central America. At last, in Costa Rica, Columbus struck gold. He discovered gold fields in which ore lay on top of the ground. His men could dig for gold with their bare hands!

Columbus decided to build a settlement near the gold fields. But once again he encountered trouble with the natives. Upon learning that the Indians were planning a raid, he attacked first. He took many hostages, including the Indians' chief.

Not long after this, Columbus had a frightening experience. It happened one day when some of his crew sailed inland to get water and supplies. The admiral remained behind with the other ships at the river's mouth. That afternoon, he heard shouting upriver, followed by guns and shooting. Then everything became strangely quiet. By nightfall, Columbus saw dead bodies floating down the river. They were the bodies of his crew.

Alone and frightened, the admiral did not know what to do. He climbed up the highest mast on the ship and frantically yelled, "Help me! Someone please help me!"

Columbus later fell asleep in his cabin. While he was sleeping, a Voice spoke to him!

"O foolish man," the Voice said. "How slow you are to serve your God! He has watched over you since you were born. He gave you the Indies and the keys to the Ocean Sea. You have gained fame among all Christians. Turn back to Him. Admit your mistakes. His mercy is infinite."

The Voice was kind and gentle. Columbus knew it spoke the truth. When he awoke, he cried. But sadly, Columbus did not heed its words. He continued searching for gold. It seemed gold was all that mattered to him.

Columbus returned to Spain. He was now fifty-three years old and in bad health. [On Ascension Day, 1506, Columbus received the last rites of the Roman Catholic Church. Then he went to be forever with the Savior whose name he carried.]

✠   ✠   ✠

Christopher Columbus had put gold before God. But God still used him to open the door for the Gospel to enter the New World. God's plan had begun. Now this new land needed to hear the message of Christ. It was time for God to send others.

CHAPTER THREE

And the light shines in the darkness; and the darkness did not comprehend it. (John 1:5)

MARTYRS FOR JESUS

During the sixteenth century, many Spanish ships crossed the ocean to the New World. But they did not come to spread the Gospel of Jesus. These early explorers sailed to America to conquer land and discover riches. They cheated the Indians and stole from them. They raided the land and murdered many of its inhabitants. The North American continent continued in darkness. It still needed the Light of Christ to brighten it.

Where was God during this century? Had He forgotten His plan? How did He spread His light into this spiritually dark land?

As you will see, God was still present, and He had not forgotten His plan. God's Holy Spirit was moving quietly through the New World. And He was using some very special people to help Him.

✦ ✦ ✦

In the 1500s, Spanish explorers took Franciscan and Dominican monks with them to Central America. The explorers brought them for encouragement and prayer. But these monks were very different from the Spanish crews and passengers. They were men of God. When the ships landed, they began to spread the Gospel of Jesus.

The monks were Christian men who had given up everything they owned to enter a group called a religious order. The men lived in a special community called a monastery. There they devoted themselves to prayer, study, and work. They separated themselves from ordinary life. Some had come from rich families. Others were from poor families. Some were well educated while others were not. In the monastery, they worked together as brothers in the Lord.

Monks knew the cost of discipleship. Because of this, they were well suited to come to the New World. Satan could not easily tempt them with riches and glory. Their hearts were not weakened by pride or fear. God knew they would remain steadfast no matter what. He knew they would obey Him and follow His call. So He sent them to North America to bring word of His Son.

After the monks arrived, they established mission towns where life was simple and peaceful. They set up churches and schools. They built homes for orphans. Everything centered around the church. The Spaniards and Indians learned to live together. They learned to trust one another, and the Indians learned about the love of Jesus. The mission towns became dots of God's light in the dark, new land.

As these men worked in the New World, they grew to love it. Riding on horseback, the monks traveled across the desert.

They enjoyed the beautiful landscape. They experienced the quiet. They watched the desert change colors. They discovered new places, and their hearts yearned to see more. Some of them became very famous explorers.

The first Spaniard to explore what is now the United States was Friar Marcos de Niza. He traveled into the New Mexico area in 1539. More missionaries followed. Hostile Indians killed some of them, but others soon took their place. By 1630, this area had twenty-five mission towns, and the friars had baptized eighty thousand Indians.

The monks continued exploring. They traveled up the West Coast. A Franciscan monk founded San Diego and San Francisco in California. The monks journeyed east. A French missionary founded the first mission in the present state of Arizona. Slowly but surely, the light of Christ was penetrating the New World.

During this time, Spanish explorers also traveled to the eastern coast of North America. In 1513, Ponce de Leon sailed to Florida. The Spanish settled Saint Augustine. They tried to settle other areas too, but the extreme heat and the fierce Seminole Indians stopped them. God did not bless the Spanish explorers as they tried to settle along the eastern coast. He had plans for pilgrims from another country to come later.

Soon missionaries from other European countries arrived in the New World. Jesuits from France journeyed to the northeast. These Jesuits were young scholars and disciples from an order called the Society of Jesus. They had vowed to follow the Lord Jesus. They had promised to remain faithful to one another as brothers in the Lord. The Jesuits were

Christian "soldiers" who practiced strong discipline and had a heart for missions.

In 1534, a Jesuit navigator named Jacques Cartier discovered the Saint Lawrence River. This river flowed eight hundred miles from west to east through Canada. Today, part of it forms a border between Canada and the United States. In the 1500s, the Algonquin and Iroquois Indians lived there.

Jacques Cartier's canoe glided silently through the waters of the Saint Lawrence River. It was an early morning in the summer of 1535. A heavy mist hung over the water. The explorer could hear the crickets singing in the pine forests. Once in a while, he heard the hoot of an owl.

This is God's country, he thought to himself. *God Himself has created this beauty for His people to enjoy. Now He has sent me to bring news of His Son to the natives.*

Cartier reached the end of the river. He entered a bay which he named the Gulf of Saint Lawrence, and he pulled his canoe onto the grassy bank. Then he set out through the forest to find wood.

"I'm going to build a cross," he said. "Yes, a great big cross. It'll bring glory to my Lord's name."

Cartier built a large thirty-foot cross to proclaim the message of salvation. He ministered to the Indians along the river, talking with them about the Lord and sharing the Gospel.

The Jesuits traveled through what would become Maine and Nova Scotia. They journeyed to the Great Lakes and the Mississippi valley. Unlike the Spanish explorers, these men treated the Indians with respect. They honored their customs and spread the love of Jesus.

Jacques Marquette was another famous Jesuit missionary. In May 1673, he and Louis Joliet canoed down the mighty Mississippi River. The Mississippi is the longest river in the United States. It begins in Minnesota and flows into the Gulf of Mexico. In 1673, a number of Indian tribes lived along its borders. The Illinois Indians camped along the northern banks, and the Chickasaw and Natchez Indians lived along its southern banks.

Marquette worked and lived with the Illinois Indians. When he died, the Illinois were very sad because they had loved him a great deal. The Indians formed a parade of thirty canoes to carry his body back to the other Jesuits. They wanted to honor this great man of God.

Another famous Jesuit missionary was Jean de Brébeuf. For nineteen years, he worked with the Huron Indians in Ontario, Canada. In 1649, the Iroquois Indians attacked one of the Huron towns.

The missionary was kneeling beside an injured Huron boy during the attack.

"Watch out, Father de Brébeuf!" one Huron yelled.

Father de Brébeuf looked behind him. Riding toward him on a black pony was an Iroquois warrior. He wore red and white paint on his face and held a tomahawk in his hand. The Indian was whooping and hollering. Father de Brébeuf stood up and faced the Indian. Then he looked toward heaven. The Indian leaned down and grabbed the priest, pulling him up onto the horse. The missionary had been captured.

The Iroquois Indians hated Father de Brébeuf, and they hated his religion. So they tortured him.

"This is your baptism," one Iroquois cursed. "Can your

Savior save you now?"

Father de Brébeuf kept silent.

"You must scream! We'll make you scream!" the Iroquois yelled.

But he did not scream, and the Indians finally killed him.

Father de Brébeuf was a martyr for Jesus. He showed the Iroquois Indians he was willing to die for his faith. He made the Indians think about the true God, and Satan was not happy about it. Satan does not like Christian martyrs. They remind him of Christ who was willing to die for others. They remind him of the victory of the cross. It is no wonder Satan had the Indians torture the missionary as they did. Satan wanted him to look weak, but Father de Brébeuf remained strong.

Another French Jesuit priest was Isaac Jogues who helped Father de Brébeuf. In 1642, Father Jogues had to travel to Quebec to get supplies. On his return, the Iroquois attacked his group. The priest escaped.

I cannot leave the Iroquois souls to be lost, he said to himself. *I must go back and win them to Christ. If I suffer for the Lord Jesus, then I suffer. He died for me. I can do no less for Him. I will go back.*

Father Jogues returned to his captors, and the Iroquois tortured him. A year later, he escaped again. He traveled back to France where he became a national hero. But Father Jogues longed to return to the New World and serve the Iroquois.

Father Jogues did return to America, where he founded the "Mission of Martyrs." Later he, like Jean de Brébeuf, became a martyr for Jesus.

✛   ✛   ✛

During the sixteenth century, many missionaries died for Jesus. These men brought God's Light into a land dark with sin. They spread this Light into the Southwest and the Northeast. They lived their lives as witnesses to the love of Jesus. Many faced the darkness of unbelief, torture, and death. But this darkness did not overcome them. They remained faithful to God and to His call upon their lives.

The Light of Christ was beginning to shine, but it was still dim. Whom would God send next?

CHAPTER

FOUR

A faithful man will abound with blessings, but he
who makes haste to be rich will not go unpunished.
(Proverbs 28:20)

WITHOUT GOD'S BLESSING

Spain became the most powerful nation on earth during the 1500s. Her ships returned from the New World filled with gold. England, France, Portugal, and Holland jealously watched Spain fill her treasury.

By 1558, Spain had settled Mexico and Central America. Portugal had colonies in Brazil, and the French had gone into northeastern Canada. No country had yet claimed the vast eastern coast of North America. When Elizabeth I became Queen of England, she decided it was time for England to colonize the New World, too.

But the first Englishmen who came to America did not come to spread the Gospel of Christ. They had other ideas in mind. Would God bless the efforts of men whose hearts were not committed to Him?

✦ ✦ ✦

In 1585, Sir Walter Raleigh sent the first English colonists to Roanoke Island off the coast of North Carolina. When food supplies got low, Governor John White sailed back to England for emergency relief. He left behind his daughter and new-born granddaughter, Virginia Dare, the first white child born in America. Two years later, White returned.

The governor and his crew approached the island in a long-boat. All was quiet. Stepping ashore, White noticed that the main gate to the palisade was open.

"Sir, this is all very strange," one crew member said. "No one is coming out to greet us."

"Look at the houses," another added. "They need repair. It's as if no one has been here for a long time. Where is every-body?"

There were no signs of life. A pale winter sun shone on the deserted settlement. The only sound was the sound of the wind stirring the dune grass.

"Look at this!" a sailor called out. Governor White and the others rushed over to find four letters carved in the trunk of a tree: C R O A.

What did it mean? Had the colonists gone to join friendly Indians on Croatan Island? The mystery was never solved, and to this day no one knows the fate of those first English settlers.

This was not a good beginning for England. For a long time, no one tried to settle another colony. Then, one of Raleigh's captains, Bartholomew Gosnold, decided to try again. Gosnold formed the Virginia Company to raise money for the new colony. This Company told everyone that the colony was a missionary outreach. King James and the clergy supported the cause. Money to finance the venture started coming in.

In December 1606, three ships set sail for North America with 144 men on board. Two weeks after sailing, bad weather forced the ships to return to port. More winter storms delayed them for months. It appeared that God was not blessing their voyage.

Was this truly a missionary outreach? Were these the people God had chosen to build His new Israel in America? No, they were not. These were not missionaries. They were not even Christian families. They were adventurers with one thing on their minds: to find gold.

After a stormy crossing, the men arrived at their destination. On May 14, 1607, they landed on a small peninsula in the James River in Virginia. That night, Captain Newport opened a sealed box containing the names of the seven men who would govern the colony. They were Captain Newport, Bartholomew Gosnold, Edward-Maria Wingfield, John Smith, John Ratcliffe, John Martin, and George Kendall.

But this council got off to a bad start, too. The seven council members refused to cooperate with one another. As soon as they set foot on land, they began to argue.

"This small peninsula is fine," said Kendall. "Let's build the settlement here."

"No," Gosnold replied, "we should look for higher ground. We need fresh water. The water is bad here. We've got to have open, clear land for planting. This place is surrounded by swamps."

"You're wrong, Gosnold," John Martin cut in. "This is good enough. We can unload here. We don't need to move."

The men decided to stay and they named the peninsula Jamestown. But they should have listened to Gosnold. They should have chosen not to stay. While beautiful in May, Jamestown became hot and humid in summer. The nearby swamps harbored mosquitoes, and these mosquitoes carried diseases. By July, almost every one of the men was sick. And this was just the beginning of their troubles.

The colonists soon had their first encounter with the local Indians. A peaceful tribe named the Perspahegh Indians lived around the Chesapeake Bay. When the Jamestown settlers accused the Indians of stealing, the two sides clashed. The Indians killed one settler and wounded another. Once again, the colonists had gotten off to a bad start.

Another problem for these settlers was their unwillingness to work. Many of the settlers were "Gentlemen," wealthy Englishmen who had never worked. Chopping wood and planting corn were jobs for commoners. In fact, a Gentleman would rather die than work—and many of them did.

On Sundays, Reverend Robert Hunt held outdoor services under an old sail. He nailed a plank between two trees for the altar. He celebrated Holy Communion and preached about trusting God. He tried to call the proud Gentlemen to repentance.

"We're all laborers in the same vineyard," Hunt preached. "Let us work together. God will provide. We must trust Him and let Him guide us."

The Gentlemen did not like this. They were not laborers.

Hunt continued. "Let us remember that we're all brothers in Christ. Whether rich or poor, we are united as one body."

And Hunt practiced what he preached. He did more than

his share of physical work. He took charge of building Jamestown's first grist mill for grinding corn. He cleaned and fed the sick. He also prayed with the settlers and talked to them about Jesus.

One of the seven council members was Captain John Smith. Though a capable leader, Smith had a bad temper. He did not get along well with others, and he liked to draw his sword to settle arguments. When the colony was almost out of food, Smith left to trade with the Indians.

He traveled up the Chickahominy River. But he was captured after killing two Indians in a fight. The warriors took him to their chief, Powhatan.

It was a warm fall afternoon. The sun's bright rays filtered through the tall fir trees. Powhatan sat in a hut made of branches. Several hundred braves surrounded him. They had painted faces, and wore feathers in their headbands. The chief wore a coonskin coat and sat on big leather pillows.

Smith knew he was in trouble. He pulled the compass out of his pocket and quickly spoke in the Indians' language.

"Chief Powhatan," Smith stammered, "here you see an instrument with great magical powers. The spirit inside this needle always seeks the North Star."

Smith held up the compass. Powhatan stared at it but did not say a word.

"You see," Smith said with more confidence, "the world is round, and on the other side of it are white chiefs. Their many ships could fill the Chickahominy River all the way to its mouth. Soon, one of these chiefs will come to look for me."

Powhatan sat up higher on the cushions. Smith knew he was listening.

"The great white father, Newport, will arrive soon. And he will have mighty guns that roar and can knock down trees standing three fields away. It is not a good idea to kill me, Most Honored Chief Powhatan."

Powhatan leaned back. Amazingly, he decided to spare Smith's life. Smith later claimed that Powhatan's daughter, Pocahontas, had helped rescue him. He said that she stopped her father from dashing Smith's head on a rock. Smith was known for tall tales, so this may not have been true. But it *was* true that Smith returned to Jamestown, carrying a gift of corn from Powhatan.

This gift reached the settlement just in time. The settlers were beginning to get hungry. There was very little food. Had it not been for the kindness of the Perspahegh, the colonists would have starved to death that first winter. God in His mercy moved on the hearts of the Indians. For some reason, God wanted Jamestown to survive. The colony struggled through the winter of 1607. But by February, only 30 of the original 144 men remained alive.

Slowly, word of the terrible conditions at Jamestown leaked back to England. The Virginia Company published sermons and letters to support the New World venture. It had to cover up the truth. In his book *True Relations*, John Smith wrote that the hardest work was over. All they needed to do now was to win souls to Christ. The words were not true, but the Virginia Company let everyone think they were. And the people believed the lie.

The Company sent more ships over, and these ships brought more settlers. But the struggling colony was not prepared for more men. It could hardly support the few it had. They had to feed the new arrivals from the common storehouse which had very little food. The new arrivals were sick and weakened by the long voyage. The colony could hardly stand the strain.

These newcomers felt it, too. They had expected to find a settlement filled with houses and activity. What they found was a group of flimsy huts enclosed by a crude, triangular fence. A huge swamp surrounded the settlement. Skinny, dirty men with bony hands and hollow cheeks greeted them. These men wore ragged clothes. Some were barefoot. Some even had the look of death.

By April 1608, the settlers had consumed Powhatan's gift of corn. That spring, the Indians planted corn, but the Jamestown colonists did not. They were not interested in planting. They had more important things to do—such as finding gold.

Captain Newport's arrival from England sparked fresh interest in gold. Five gold experts returned with him. The Virginia Company had sent them after the first sample of ore turned out to be "fool's gold." These so-called experts declared that Jamestown rested on a foundation of gold! Everyone started digging. Soon Newport sailed off with another cargo of ore, but this proved to be worthless, too.

When he returned from this trip, Newport brought back seventy new settlers. However, he failed to return with extra food, tools, or supplies. By December 1608, the food shortage was critical. Captain Smith stepped in.

"The Indians are starving us to death!" Smith complained. "I'm going to get that Powhatan if it's the last thing I do!"

This hateful attitude was no help. In fact, it was a miracle that the Indians had shared their corn at all. Powhatan was probably the only chief along the east coast who would put up with Smith's behavior or trade with him. Many hostile Indians lived in the New World: The fierce Iroquois hurt the French settlers in the northeast; the ferocious Seminoles kept the Spaniards from settling Florida. Yet, God directed these first English settlers to an area with a peaceful tribe!

When Smith left Jamestown to find Powhatan, peace was not on his mind.

"You do not need to come to me with guns and swords, Captain Smith," Powhatan said. "I will trade with you."

"This is good," Smith replied. "I'll return tomorrow to trade."

But Smith did not intend to trade. He intended to take. He arranged a secret signal with his men so he could capture the chief. But Smith could not fool Powhatan. The chief slipped away leaving Smith and his men to fight his Indian warriors.

The lack of food remained a problem. In April 1609, the colonists discovered that rats had eaten their last store of food. Now the colony had nothing at all! Immediately, everyone left. Some moved to the oyster banks to live on shellfish. Others journeyed upriver to hunt for acorns and berries. Some sought help from Powhatan, who took them in. More than half of them died, including Reverend Hunt, the only man of God.

Why did the council not simply relocate the entire settlement? The summer heat was terrible, and the swamp gave them diseases. And during their second year, nine out of every ten men died. Why did they stay? The answer is that they did not seek the Lord's direction. They did not turn to Him for help. And they certainly did not evangelize the natives. These settlers were not men of God. They chose their own way, and they suffered for it.

Back in England, the Virginia Company was not seeking God either. It was still trying to cover up the truth. Knowing things were not going well, it wrote a new charter and set up a government with a single governor.

This new governor, Thomas Gates, set sail in May 1609. Nine English vessels sped toward the New World. They carried five hundred passengers, including the first women and children. Governor Gates sailed in the flagship *Sea Venture.*

During a hurricane, the nine ships were separated. One went down and one turned back. The *Sea Venture* landed safely on the island of Bermuda. The other six ships limped on to Jamestown, disobeying strict orders to meet in Bermuda.

Had they obeyed, the fleet could have rested in Bermuda. The people could have eaten good food and recovered from the hurricane. As it happened four hundred sick, helpless, and starving passengers arrived at Jamestown harbor. The little settlement could not care for them. In the fall of 1609, as many died from despair as from disease.

The afternoons grew shorter and colder as winter approached. The scavengers who had left to hunt for food returned for shelter. While the first frost wiped out mosquitoes, it did not wipe out the hunger. Jamestown had no food. It entered its "starving time."

The colonists ate anything they could find. They consumed the livestock and cats and dogs. They even ate rats and mice.

They dug up the roots of trees and bushes. They gnawed on shoe leather and leather straps. They devoured boiled book covers. Many froze to death because they were too weak to stand up. Only sixty people survived.

In May 1610, Gates arrived in a ship named *Deliverance.* Only sixty shabby, skinny figures met him. Gates was so horrified that he decided to abandon the settlement. But another ship carrying a new governor dropped anchor. And this governor ordered everyone to stay. God had moved to save the first colony in Virginia.

Over time, conditions improved. Then, something delightful happened which showed God at last might be bestowing grace on the Virginia Company.

It began when Pocahontas was kidnapped by the settlers and held for ransom. Governor Thomas Dale told Powhatan to pay the ransom in corn. Powhatan paid. When Dale demanded more corn, Powhatan would not pay. Dale organized a war party.

In the meantime, a young colonist named John Rolfe asked Governor Dale for permission to marry the young Indian princess. Surprisingly, Dale agreed and so did Powhatan. Hate turned into joy. This was the first wedding between a white man and an Indian.

Rolfe and his new bride sailed to England. Pocahontas later died of pneumonia, and her grieving husband returned to Virginia alone.

Back in the Colony, he began to experiment with a new crop. This crop was tobacco, the first cash crop in the New World.

By 1622, more than twelve hundred settlers lived on ten widely scattered plantations in Virginia. Yet the colony only had three ministers to preach the Gospel.

The Virginia Company finally sold its ownership to a group of ten adventurers. These men established a system of independent rule in the colony. Two representatives from each plantation met to make laws. This was the first representative assembly in North America. It was a new start for Virginia.

The people who settled Jamestown considered themselves good Christians. Yet they tried to settle the colony without God! They did not seek His guidance. They did not ask His forgiveness. And they did not receive His blessings.

However, the next group of settlers knew better than to start a new life without Christ. The next people who came to America did trust God, and it made a big difference.

CHAPTER
FIVE

For the Lord your God is bringing you into a good land. (Deuteronomy 8:7)

TO THE PROMISED LAND

On a warm, hazy July morning in 1620, three barges floated down a canal in Holland. They were on their way from Leyden to the seaport town of Delftshaven. In the distance was a large, stone windmill with its white sails slowly turning. Field crickets chirped in the low, green fields that lined the canal. Everyone stood silently.

At last the time had come—they were beginning their long journey to the New World.

Who were these people and where were they going? Why were they leaving Holland? Was this another group of settlers like those who had gone to Jamestown? Or were these people different?

These people would be known as Pilgrims. Unlike the Jamestown settlers, they were people of God. They were Christians who lived in commitment to Jesus Christ. They sought His will in everything they did. And God blessed them every step of the way.

✝ ✝ ✝

The Church of England was England's national church. It was a Protestant church, run by the House of Bishops. The head of this church was the English monarch. During the 1600s, many people believed that reform was needed in this church. They wanted it to be run according to the Bible. They desired the worship services to include Bible reading and personal prayers. They wished to do away with many of the rituals used by the church.

Two groups of people sought such change. The first group remained loyal to the church, but they still wanted to purify it. They were called the Puritans. The second and smaller group was called the Separatists. They believed the church would not change, so they "separated" themselves from it and began their own worship services.

The House of Bishops did not fear the Puritans. They simply kept them from holding positions of authority within the church. The Separatists, however, were another matter. The Bishops saw them as a threat. If other groups followed, the Bishops would lose control of the church. They did not want this to happen, so they persecuted the Separatists, and the Separatists left England.

In the village of Scrooby, England, lived a young Separatist named William Bradford. Bradford's congregation traveled to Holland where they could worship in peace. But life in the new country was very hard. As poor immigrants, the Separatists had to work twelve to fifteen hours a day. Their children were unhappy and often tempted by worldly values. The Separatists sought the Lord's guidance.

"I'm beginning to think God wants us to travel to the New World," said Bradford.

"I think you're right, William," replied Pastor John Robinson. "But there is more to it than just traveling."

"What do you mean, Pastor?" asked Bradford.

"Well, I believe God is telling us to go, but He is sending us for a special reason. He wants us to build a living temple for the Lord in the new land. It is to be a spiritual temple. Our lives are to shine as His Light in a dark world."

God's plan for America continued. He was guiding these Separatists, and they were hearing His call.

But getting across the Atlantic was not easy. They needed money to pay for the ship and the voyage. They needed food supplies to last them until they could harvest a crop. In addition, they needed a fishing vessel so they could set up a trade in the New World. Where would they find the funds?

They found them through a London merchant named Thomas Weston. Weston represented a group of adventurers in London who had heard about the Separatists and wanted to help them. The Separatists entered an agreement with the adventurers to work for seven years and pay back the loan.

The Separatists sold their houses and prepared for the journey. They bought an old freighter named the *Speedwell*. This ship would pick them up at Delftshaven and take them to Southampton, England. There they would join a larger ship named the *Mayflower*. Since the *Speedwell* was small, Pastor Robinson and some of the congregation remained behind. William Brewster, an elder, became acting pastor until Robinson could join them.

The time came to leave. Robinson declared a day of fasting and prayer to prepare them spiritually for the journey. At the end of the day, they enjoyed a farewell dinner together, singing hymns and Psalms. The next morning, they boarded the barge which would take them to Delftshaven.

Bradford stood on the barge and looked back at the broad, low fields near Leyden. He watched the windmills turning in the breeze.

"This is an important thing we're doing today," he said to his wife Dorothy. "We're making a pilgrimage to a distant land. We are now Pilgrims following their Lord."

"I know, William," Dorothy replied. "And God will bless that which we are about to do."

They reached Delftshaven, and on July 22, 1620, the *Speedwell* headed to Southampton to join the *Mayflower*. The *Mayflower* carried about eighty "strangers," people who were not Separatists. Some shared the Separatists' feelings about the Church of England. Others sailed to the New World for adventure and riches. None of the passengers were Gentlemen.

It was time to leave. Suddenly, Thomas Weston barged in, carrying a contract in his hand.

"Elder Brewster, your people must sign this contract!" Weston ordered as he shoved the document into Brewster's hand.

"We will not, sir," Brewster calmly replied. "You have changed the terms. We will not agree to this."

"Then you will suffer," Weston snapped. "Be gone with all of you! I'll not pay another farthing on your debts!"

With that, Weston stormed off the ship. He returned to

London, refusing to pay off their final debts. The Separatists had to sell many casks of butter to repay their creditors.

On August 5, 1620, they finally set sail for the New World. But the *Speedwell* began having trouble, and both vessels returned to port twice. The first time, they headed back to Southampton. The second time, they returned to Plymouth and sold the problem freighter. Everyone crowded onto the *Mayflower*.

Why had God let this happen? Was He really calling these people to the New World? Yes, He was. Bradford recorded in his journal that God had a reason for this. After the freighter broke down, twenty passengers decided not to accompany them to America. This trouble with the *Speedwell* united the Separatists and the "strangers." God knew they would need to be united. Much awaited them on the other side of the ocean. Like Gideon's army in ancient Israel, God needed only a few to complete His work.

For seven weeks the Pilgrims huddled in the damp and dark below decks. (This was an area about the size of a volleyball court.) All hatches had to be battened down because of the stormy weather. The area smelled bad because of the bilge water and lack of fresh air. They could eat only dried foods, and no one could cook. The children had no place to play. Yet the Pilgrims did not complain. They trusted God.

And God was taking care of them. Only two lives were lost during the entire trip, and neither of these was a Pilgrim. One was a sailor who did not like the Pilgrims and gloated at their seasickness. He delighted in telling them how much he looked forward to feeding their dead bodies to the fish. But this sailor suddenly came down with an unknown fever. No one else caught the mysterious disease, and the sailor died within a single day! After that, the crew did not mock the Pilgrims anymore. A servant named William Butten also died. He had refused to drink the sour lemon juice which prevented scurvy. This disobedience cost him his life.

Another passenger almost lost his life. This was John Carver's servant, John Howland.

"I can't stand it down here, sir," Howland complained. "It stinks. I must get some fresh air!"

"You may not leave," Carver replied. "The captain has forbid any of us from going topside. It's too dangerous in this storm."

Howland could stand it no longer. He decided to climb up and go onto the main deck anyway. It was a nightmare outside! Howland had never seen anything like it. Violent winds shrieked, tearing at the masts and sails. Stormy, black clouds covered the sky. Huge waves pitched the small ship from side to side. Raindrops beat the deck and stung Howland's face.

All of a sudden, the ship seemed to drop out from beneath him. Howland plunged into the icy water. Instantly, the frightened man blindly reached out. Amazingly, a line from one of the ship's masts happened to be trailing in the water. The rope twirled around Howland's wrist, and he gripped it with all his might. When he was finally hauled aboard the *Mayflower*, the poor man's skin had turned blue. The servant soon recovered, but he never again stuck his head above the deck until invited to do so.

During another storm, giant waves tossed the *Mayflower* from side to side. The ship rolled so far over on her sides that the alarmed passengers feared she might lose her cargo. The lantern in the space 'tween decks swung sharply from side to side. Suddenly, a loud boom thundered through the ship.

"What was that?" Elizabeth Winslow asked her husband as she tried to calm a frightened child. "It sounded terrible!"

"Watch out, everyone!" a sailor warned as he dashed in. "The crossbeam that supports the main mast has cracked! It could give way any minute!"

The men swarmed around it, trying to lift it back into place. They could not budge it. From the look on the captain's face, the Pilgrims knew the situation was serious.

"We must pray, Captain," announced William Bradford. "God can save us."

And pray they did. All at once, Brewster got an idea.

"My printing press!" he exclaimed. "I have a great iron screw in my printing press! That screw could hold up the beam. It's on board somewhere. We must find it!"

The screw Brewster wanted was the large one used to press type with ink onto pages of paper. That was why the machine was called a printing press. The men began a frantic search for the press.

"I've found it!" someone yelled.

The men hauled it into place and cranked it up.

"Slowly now," Brewster directed. "It must meet the beam."

The wood groaned and creaked. Slowly, the huge screw lifted the beam back into place. The sailor and the Pilgrims joined together to praise God.

Later, the Pilgrims questioned Captain Jones.

"Captain," John Carver asked, "should we go on? Can the *Mayflower* make it to America?"

"Yes," the seaman answered thoughtfully, "I think she can make it. We're closer to the New World than to England anyway. She's still sound in the water. She can get us there."

"Land ho! Land ho!" shouted the sailor from the crow's nest. Everyone rushed up to the main deck to catch a first glimpse of the new land. They saw a long stretch of coastline covered with dune grass and scrub pine. The date was November 9, 1620.

"Captain, the fishermen call this place Cape Cod," announced the pilot. "But we're not far off course. We can turn south and be at the Hudson River in just a few days."

But strong headwinds and fierce tides made going south treacherous and almost impossible. After three days, the Pilgrims began to wonder what was happening.

"Is it possible God doesn't want us to sail into the Hudson?" Winslow asked.

"It may be," replied Bradford.

"Perhaps He has blown us off course on purpose," added Brewster. "Perhaps He wants us to remain here."

After much prayer and discussion, the Pilgrims instructed Captain Jones to turn back. On November 11, they dropped anchor at Cape Cod.

But now a new problem arose.

"If we settle here," Bradford said thoughtfully, "we'll no longer be under the authority of the Virginia Company. Since we don't have a charter from the New England Company, we'll be under the authority of no one."

"William is right," Winslow quickly agreed. "We need some form of government. We don't want rebellion on our hands."

The Pilgrim leadership agreed that they had to act quickly. On the afternoon of November 11, 1620, the Pilgrims signed the Mayflower Compact. This historic moment was the first time that free and equal men had ever entered a covenant to create a new society, based on biblical principles. One of these principles was that all men are created equal in the sight of God. A second was that a government must only govern people who agree to submit to it. These two important principles became the cornerstones of America's constitutional government.

✢ ✢ ✢

The Pilgrims began their journey by kneeling on the dock at Delftshaven to ask God's blessing. They ended it on the sands of Cape Cod, kneeling to thank Him for the blessing of safe passage.

With winter storms howling around the tip of the Cape, the Pilgrims turned their eyes toward heaven. Behind them was the mighty ocean they had just crossed. Before them lay a wild and savage land. What could sustain these people now but the Spirit of God and His grace?

CHAPTER
SIX

Thou didst provide bread from heaven for them for their hunger, Thou didst bring forth water from a rock for them for their thirst. (Nehemiah 9:15)

FIVE KERNELS OF CORN

The Pilgrims were strangers in a strange land. What was this place called Cape Cod? In winter, it appeared bleak and windswept. Dark, thick underbrush clung to its low hills. A bitter cold, northwest wind pounded the steep sand dunes.

Sixteen men rowed ashore in the ship's boat to find firewood and explore. As the afternoon light began to fail, they returned. Everyone crowded onto the main deck. As it happened, the men ashore had found something. They had discovered thirty-six ears of corn buried in a large iron pot. The Pilgrims were greatly encouraged. Yet little did they realize how important this particular food would become to their lives in the New World.

✝ ✝ ✝

For three weeks, the Pilgrims assembled a sailing shallop. This was a small, open boat with oars and a sail. On December 6, 1620, ten of their chief men and a few seamen set out to explore the coast around the Cape.

The first afternoon, the explorers spied some Indians cutting up a beached whale. The Indians ran away before they could signal them. The second night, they built a barricade of cut branches to protect them from the wind on shore and from any Indians. They tried to sleep, but they kept hearing Indian cries in the distance. Just before dawn, the men got up for prayer and breakfast. Suddenly, bloodcurdling screams pierced the morning calm.

"Indians, Indians!" one of the men yelled.

Dozens of arrows showered the camp. The men fired two muskets from behind the barricade. More arrows flew in, accompanied by whooping and hollering. Several Pilgrims rushed from behind the barricade and discharged their muskets. The Indians shrieked and quickly scattered. The relieved explorers gathered to thank God for safely delivering them.

The men returned to the shallop and continued south along the inner shore of the Cape. Their pilot, Robert Coppin, told them about a good harbor farther along at the mouth of a creek. However, around one o'clock in the afternoon, snow began to fall. The shallop sailed right past the harbor! As the day wore on, the wind picked up, and the sea became rough. The boat's rudder broke. As the storm worsened, the men tried to haul in the sail. But they broke the mast in three pieces, and the sail fell overboard.

"I don't know where we are," Coppin moaned. "Lord, have mercy on us!"

By now, the tide was pushing them toward shore. The shallop was headed straight toward a cove full of breakers.

Suddenly, seaman Clark yelled, "Come about fast, or the waves will swamp us!"

The men rowed furiously, saving the shallop from the very edge of the breakers. Finally, they found shelter on the lee side of a small island. This was the side away from the wind. The explorers named the island after seaman Clark and spent a wet, miserable night on it.

The next day was Sunday. A bright morning sun greeted the men. They decided to rest and keep the Sabbath. On Monday, the explorers began a day filled with amazing discoveries.

"Look at this!" Bradford said excitedly. "This island is in the midst of a large harbor!"

"And there's the mainland over there," Captain Standish announced, pointing west.

"You know," Coppin said, "this harbor looks deep enough to take ships. I think the *Mayflower* could anchor here!"

The men rowed the shallop across to the mainland. There they found that the land sloped gently up from the water's edge. The soil was rich and fertile. The explorers stumbled upon four creeks with the sweetest-tasting water they had ever tasted. And finally, they found twenty acres of land already cleared. It was an ideal place to build a settlement. Happier than they had been in weeks, the excited men hurried back to the *Mayflower*.

The Pilgrims named the site after Plymouth, England. Immediately, they began to build. First, they laid out the main street. Then they constructed the palisade, a large wooden fence. Finally, they assembled the common house, where they would stay until their homes were built.

That first winter in Plymouth was hard. Although the weather was bitter cold, the Pilgrims worked on their town. They cut down trees and stacked heavy logs. They trudged through the snow and slept on the damp ground. The work was difficult, and they were not physically strong. Three months at sea had left them weak. Many became sick and died. At one point, two or three people were dying each day. By winter's end, the Pilgrims had lost fifty-one people—half their number!

But these people were not like other settlers. The harder things got, the more they prayed and trusted God. Satan could not break their spirits. He could not get them to give in to despair and self-pity. They knew their Heavenly Father would see them through. . . and He did.

Winter passed and the Pilgrims welcomed spring. One day in March, the men gathered in the common house while Miles Standish demonstrated military tactics. Suddenly, they heard a shout, "Indian coming!" Indian coming? Surely he meant *Indians* coming. Captain Standish shook his head and looked out the window. He saw a tall, well-built Indian walking up the main road toward the common house. The men inside hurried to the door where the Indian stopped.

"Welcome!" he suddenly boomed, in a deep voice.

The startled Pilgrims could not say a word. This Indian spoke English! Finally, they managed to reply, "Welcome."

Everyone gathered around the stranger as he spoke.

"My name is Samoset," the Indian said. "I am from the Algonquin tribe to the north. I love to travel. I came here with Captain Thomas Dermer, the English sea captain who is exploring this area for the Council for New England."

"Yes," Bradford broke in. "We're applying to the Council for a patent for this land."

"Tell us, Samoset, how did you learn English?' Brewster inquired.

"From fishing captains who put in to the Maine shore," the Indian answered.

"What can you tell us about the other Indians?" Winslow asked.

Samoset then related a story which caused everyone to thank God. Until 1617, a large, hostile tribe, named the Patuxets, had lived in the territory. These Indians hated the white man. Four years before the Pilgrims' arrival, a strange disease had killed every man, woman, and child in the tribe. Neighboring tribes shunned the area now, convinced that some supernatural spirit had destroyed the Patuxets.

"So the Patuxets cleared the land!" exclaimed Bradford.

"Yes," answered Samoset. "I'm now staying with the Wampanoags who live fifty miles from here. Their chief, Massasoit, rules over a number of small tribes in the area."

"But who attacked us on the beach?" Standish asked.

"That must have been the Nausets. A few years ago, a captain named Thomas Hunt stole some Nauset warriors and sold them as slaves. The Nausets hate the white man now."

Samoset stopped. "It's late. I'll sleep here and return to Massasoit in the morning."

The Pilgrims kept a silent watch on the Indian through the night. He did not bother anyone. The next morning they gave him gifts to take to Massasoit.

The following Thursday, Samoset returned. This time, another Indian who spoke English accompanied him. But this Indian was a Patuxet!

The Pilgrims listened as this new visitor, named Squanto, told his story. In 1605, Squanto had been captured and taken to England. Nine years later, he escaped and returned to his village with an English fishing expedition. But Captain Hunt tricked him and nineteen other Patuxets to go onto his ship. The captain then sailed across the bay to kidnap the Nausets. Hunt took all the captive Indians to Spain where he sold them as slaves. Squanto was sold to Spanish monks, who took him back to their monastery and taught him about Jesus. God was preparing the Indian for the role he would play at Plymouth.

Before long, Squanto was able to return to London. In 1619, he sailed for home with Captain Dermer. Dermer picked up Samoset in Maine and dropped both of them off at Plymouth.

"When I learned that my people were dead," Squanto continued, "I went to Massasoit, who has shown me much kindness."

Surprisingly, Chief Massasoit and sixty painted warriors soon appeared at the settlement. The Pilgrims treated them royally. They blew a trumpet and beat a drum in honor of his arrival. They ushered the chief into one of the unfinished houses where they drank a toast to him. They gave him gifts. All of this pleased the chief greatly. By the time he left, he and the Pilgrims had entered into a peace treaty.

God was taking care of His children. Massasoit was a man of peace, who welcomed the Pilgrims to Cape Cod. Like Powhatan, Massasoit was probably one of the only Indian chiefs on the northeast coast of America who would have done this. But, unlike the settlers at Jamestown, the Pilgrims did not make trouble. They treated Massasoit and his warriors with respect. They showed them the love of Christ.

When Massasoit left, Squanto remained. "I would like to stay," he said. "My people are gone. I have no one now. I can teach you many things."

Squanto helped the Pilgrims in many ways. He taught them how to plant corn the Indian way so it would grow.

"First, you bury the kernels with three fish," he instructed. "The head of each fish must point inward, like the spokes in a wheel. As the fish decompose, you must guard against the wolves who'll try to steal them."

By summer, the Pilgrims had twenty full acres of corn.

Squanto taught them other valuable lessons. He showed them how to stalk deer, plant pumpkins, and make maple syrup. He told them which herbs to eat and which to use for medicine. And he introduced them to the beaver trade. Bradford wrote in his journal that Squanto was a true gift from God.

The time had come for Captain Jones to return to England. The Pilgrims stood on shore and watched the *Mayflower* sail away. Not one of them sailed back with him. Even though many had lost loved ones during the winter, they did not want to leave Plymouth. Something special had happened to them. They had suffered together in the cause of Christ. They had shared the love of Jesus with one another. Now, they were a family. They would not separate.

In May, the Pilgrims celebrated their first wedding when Edward Winslow and Susanna White married. The summer of 1621 found the Pilgrims working hard, building more houses, and trading with the Indians. That fall, they harvested more than enough crops to see them through the winter.

In October, Governor Bradford declared a day of public thanksgiving. The Pilgrims were filled with thanks—to

Squanto and the Wampanoags who had been so friendly, and to God who had delivered them from certain death. Massasoit came with ninety Indians and plenty of deer and turkeys. The Pilgrim women cooked fresh vegetables and baked fruit pies. The Indians introduced the settlers to popcorn. It was a time of prayer and games. The Pilgrims thanked God for meeting their needs. Then they competed with the Indians in shooting contests. They held wrestling matches and races. The joyous celebration lasted three days!

In November, a ship from England dropped anchor, bringing new colonists. The Pilgrims also received their charter, granted by the New England Company. In addition, Thomas Weston sent another contract so the Pilgrims could purchase more supplies. The Pilgrims agreed to his harsh terms and then spent twenty years working off the debt. They faithfully repaid every shilling they had borrowed and the interest, sometimes at a rate of thirty and fifty percent! But Satan could not pull these people into bitter arguments. They kept their eyes on Jesus and trusted Him to see them through.

During the winter of 1621-22, the Pilgrims entered a "starving time" like the settlers in Jamestown. Plymouth now had thirty-five extra people so the supplies went quickly. They were down to a daily ration of only five kernels of corn apiece. But, as always, they had a choice. They could either give in to bitterness and despair, or they could trust Jesus. They chose Jesus.

Unexpectedly, a ship put into their harbor one day on its way from Virginia back to England. While the captain had little extra food, he did have trading goods. He agreed to trade his corn for beaver pelts. The Pilgrims now had food until spring! Unlike the settlers at Jamestown, not a single person starved to death. God had taken care of the Pilgrims again.

Another year passed. It was now April 1623, and time to plant once again. The settlers needed twice as much corn this year to feed the growing colony. The ruling group of men in Plymouth decided to permit a second planting. After finishing the common cornfield, the settlers could plant corn for themselves on land of their own.

The Pilgrims worked hard and completed both plantings, but a drought came. For twelve weeks, no rain fell. Leaves of corn hung limp on the stalks. The beans looked as if they had been burned in a fire.

"The Lord is trying to tell us something," Brewster preached to the congregation. "We must look into our own hearts and humble ourselves before Him."

What was happening? The Pilgrims did not know. But they did know that the best thing to do was to turn to God. The Pilgrims began to search their hearts. Had greed taken hold of them when they planted their own crops? Had they become too self-centered? The Pilgrims waited for God to answer. The leaders declared a day of fasting and prayer.

That morning everyone gathered in the blockhouse. They spent many hours praying and praising God. By the time they left, dark clouds were seen rolling across the sky. By morning, a soft, sweet rain had begun to fall. For fourteen days, this rain gently soaked the parched earth.

That season, the Pilgrims harvested all the corn they needed for the upcoming winter. They even had extra corn to trade! God had performed another miracle for His beloved.

The Pilgrims planned a second thanksgiving. Again, the Indians joined them because they, too, recognized the hand of God in ending the drought. Laughter and games filled the colony. Tables overflowed with delicious food. And, at each plate lay five kernels of corn . . . so no one would forget God's loving care.

✢ ✢ ✢

In three years, Plymouth had become a successful colony in the New World. The Pilgrims had followed God's call. They had formed a new community of Christians in the colonies, and God had blessed them every step of the way.

At last, the Light of Christ was shining brightly on the American shore.

CHAPTER

SEVEN

Thy kingdom come,
Thy will be done,
On earth as it is in heaven. (Matthew 6:10)

THY KINGDOM COME

The Puritans knew they had to leave England. They had wanted to bring about change by working within, but the Bishops did not want reform and made such changes impossible. By 1628, many Puritans realized they had to leave.

More and more they looked to America. Why not a settlement of Puritans there, loyal to both the Church of England and the Crown? In America, they could obey the laws of God as well as the laws of men. In America, they could spread the Gospel. In America, they could try to build God's kingdom on earth.

Was it possible? Could a group of believers actually begin to set up God's kingdom on earth? Was this part of God's plan, too? The answers to these questions are *yes*. God Himself was directing the Puritans to come to the New World. He knew what lay ahead for America, and He had chosen these people to lay the foundation stones the country needed to survive.

✝   ✝   ✝

"But John, you're not a Separatist," argued Robert Ryece. "You're a Puritan! The Church needs you here. You must stay!"

John Winthrop stood at the window, staring at the fields in front of his house. How he loved this estate in Suffolk. How he loved England. Despite the bright sun's rays, Winthrop felt as though a gray fog covered the room.

"Robert, I must go," Winthrop quietly explained. "God is telling me to go. I know we're not like the Separatists, but now none of us can change the Church from within. Bishop Laud has given King Charles a list of our names. It's time to go."

Winthrop turned to look at his friend. Ryece stood beside a table, holding some papers.

"Robert," Winthrop continued, "you know how much I love the Church. But we can't change anything here. It's become too corrupt. You've read what I've written in those papers. You know what I've said."

Ryece sat down in a big leather chair. Winthrop sat in the chair beside him.

"They're asking me to go," Winthrop said. "I must. The time is right, Robert. God has set everything in motion. He's doing this because He wants us to go."

God *had* set everything in motion. King Charles had already signed the Massachusetts Bay Company Charter. The Puritans had faced enough persecution. They were ready to leave. They had grown strong through it all and were spiritually equipped to handle the hardships of building a new home. Favorable reports from the colony at Plymouth encouraged them to try.

In 1628, sixty-six Puritan men sailed with John Endecott to Salem, Massachusetts. The following year, Reverend Francis Higginson and two hundred Puritans left England to join them.

On August 26, 1629, Puritan leaders met at Cambridge, England, where many had attended the university together.

"We enter this agreement willingly," Richard Saltonstall said.

"We agree to be ready in our persons to further the work of Christ in the New World," another added.

"We'll prepare to leave by next March," Winthrop directed.

Three days later, the men elected John Winthrop to be governor. Winthrop began to arrange passage for more than a thousand Puritans who wanted to emigrate.

John Winthrop sat in his cabin as the *Arbella* sailed through the calm waters of the Atlantic. He had been praying. Carefully, he removed his writing box from the chart table. After selecting a quill pen, he dipped it into the wide-bottomed ink bottle and wiped off the excess ink.

"This love among Christians is a real thing," Winthrop wrote. "It is absolutely necessary to the well-being of the Body of Christ. . . . We are a company . . . knit together by this bond of love."

Then came the heart of his vision.

"We are entered into covenant with Him for this work. . . (W)e must be knit together in this work as one man."

Winthrop named his composition *A Model of Christian Charity*. It ranks in importance with the Mayflower Compact. The Pilgrims' agreement stated that a group of people, gathered together under God, were going to be governed by mutual consent. John Winthrop spelled out why such a government would work. It would work because the believers had entered into covenant with God and with one another. It became the definition of covenant love.

On June 8, 1630, Governor Winthrop stood at the rail of the *Arbella* and got his first glimpse of New England: the fir-covered hills of Maine. He felt the fresh, warm coastal breeze against his skin. He marveled at pine trees taller than any he had ever seen. He enjoyed the sea gulls flying overhead. Four days later, the *Arbella* approached the colony of Salem, Massachusetts.

Surely this isn't Salem! Winthrop thought as he studied the mainland. *There are only a few tents and huts here! The town must be farther back in the woods.*

As the ship drew closer, the governor realized it was Salem! He caught sight of some people walking toward the beach. They were thin and ragged-looking. Their shoulders were hunched. Something was terribly wrong.

The provisional governor, John Endecott, met Winthrop on shore. The two men talked.

"Governor Winthrop, there are only eighty-five of us left," Endecott said. "More than eighty have died, and the rest have returned to England. Others want to go home as well."

"Good heavens, man, you started with two hundred and sixty-six people!" Winthrop replied. "This is as bad as Jamestown. And these people are decent Puritans, not fortune hunters!"

"We hold a teaching service on Thursdays, and two services on Sundays. But they do no good." Endecott sighed. "The people hear the words but nothing changes."

Winthrop's mind was racing. *Is it all over?* he thought. *Will covenant love work?* Endecott interrupted Winthrop's thoughts to tell him more of the story.

During the first winter, the new settlers had been very sick. Endecott wrote Governor Bradford at Plymouth to ask for help. Bradford sent Samuel Fuller, a doctor who understood scurvy and other illnesses.

"I was prepared to dislike Fuller," Endecott offered. "After all, he is a Separatist. But he took care of us and showed us Christian love. He and I often talked at night by the fire. I learned much about what God is doing fifty miles down the coast."

"Tell me about it," Winthrop requested.

"At Plymouth, the Church influences the civil government," Endecott began, "but the two are separate. Church members choose their own leaders, and the civil government holds its own elections. We based our church here on the model at Plymouth. We elected Higginson as pastor and Skelton as teacher. We thought it would work, but—"

"That's it!" Winthrop suddenly interrupted. "That's why it's not working!"

"I don't understand," Endecott replied, with a puzzled look on his face.

"Don't you see? These Puritans love God and want to do His will. The problem is they're not living out the other part of the covenant. They're not living out their commitment to one another!"

"But the Separatists were already a church," Endecott objected. "We've just started!"

"All the more reason we've got to live up to our covenant with each other!" Winthrop stressed. "And it must begin with you and me. Unless each of us is willing to put our whole lives into the work here, we can't expect the others to."

Endecott stood up straight. "Sir," he said, "you can count on me."

Immediately, the governor made plans. "I want you to assemble every man and boy at the center of town today, one hour before noon. Have the women come, too. In the meantime, I'll see about getting my belongings ashore."

Winthrop started out the door, then abruptly turned back.

"Oh, and tell the Gentlemen—Mr. Saltonstall, Mr. Pynchon, Mr. Nowell, and the others—that this includes them as well!" Winthrop smiled. "You'd better suggest they wear old clothes," he added.

"Right, Governor," Endecott replied.

Promptly at one o'clock, Endecott walked to the center of the huts and shelters that formed the town. A number of people were already there, staring at their governor. He was dressed in boots, work pants, and an old shirt. He looked more like a servant than a Gentleman. Endecott handed him a list of names.

"The situation here is not exactly what I expected," Winthrop began.

Everyone stood still and listened.

"It's going to take a lot of hard work," the Governor continued, "but I think we can correct things. By the end of the summer, every one of you is going to be in a proper dwelling.

Until then, more than one family will have to live together, at least for the first winter."

The crowd began to murmur.

"But Governor, how are we going to do it?" one settler asked.

"By God's grace," Winthrop replied, "and by helping one another."

Just then, Richard Saltonstall and a friend strolled into the gathering, carrying on a conversation. Saltonstall wore a white shirt with a ruffled collar. Winthrop glared at them, then turned back to the others.

"First of all, who can fish?" he asked. Eight men raised their hands. Winthrop consulted Endecott. "All right, Packham and Kenworthy, each of you take three men. On alternate days, you'll take turns fishing in the shallop.

"Now, the women," he said, looking at his list. "Some of you will do field work in the mornings. The others will care for the sick with Mr. Skelton. Mr. Skelton, you'll be responsible for the food supplies, too. Be sure to let me know how much food we have in store."

Winthrop then addressed Mr. Higginson, who was sitting on a stump. "Reverend, I know you've been ill. Your job will be to pray for us and to preach on Sundays."

Winthrop handed the folded list to Endecott. "The rest of you will form two work parties. Those under forty will go with Mr. Endecott. Those over forty will come with me. Are there any questions?"

"Yes," Richard Saltonstall said as he stepped forward. "John, you don't really expect *me* to work like this, do you?"

"Yes, Richard, I do."

"But common labor, John! I brought nine men with me to do that. And you brought more men than I did!"

Winthrop hesitated. "Richard, last August, you signed an agreement at Cambridge. Do you remember?"

Saltonstall did not respond.

"You agreed to be ready to carry on this work. So did I. It won't succeed unless every man gives his all. We're all laborers in God's vineyard."

Saltonstall shook his head, almost too angry to speak. "This is—"

"This is the way it's going to be," Winthrop stated strongly. "And I'll tell you something else." The governor looked around at everyone. "I consider being late a sin against God. We're doing the work God has called us to do. We won't steal His time by being late!

"Starting tomorrow, we'll meet here promptly at two hours past sunrise for daily work assignments. Bring something with you to eat at the noon hour. We'll work until four o'clock. The rest of the day will be yours."

The people began to talk excitedly.

"Are there any more questions?"

There were none.

The fall and winter of 1630 tested the Puritans' commitment. More shiploads of settlers arrived and the food supplies dropped dangerously low. Once again, Winthrop stepped in. He traded with the local Indians for corn. Then he sent the ship, *Lyon*, home to London for supplies, with orders to use his own money to purchase them.

This kind of personal sacrifice had become his pattern. Winthrop believed that one should commit everything to the cause. Often he dug into his own funds to meet the needs of the struggling colony. In fact, he alone supported the colony for a while. And he never once complained, not even in his personal journals.

The winter months dragged on. By February, the settlers had eaten most of the corn. There was still no sign of the *Lyon*.

"God is withholding His blessing from us," Higginson preached. "We must search our hearts and humble ourselves before Him. And we must pray for a miracle."

There was nothing else they could do. By February 5, the corn was gone, the ground nuts had been consumed, and the clam banks exhausted. The *Lyon* was so long overdue that the Puritans could only think she had been shipwrecked.

They declared a day of fasting and prayer. But the day never came to pass.

"Governor!" someone yelled out. "She's back, sir. The *Lyon* is coming into port!'

Winthrop spied the ship at the harbor's mouth. Everyone ran down to shore. The *Lyon* had returned, loaded with food and supplies. Her cargo consisted of wheat, meal, peas, oatmeal, beef, pork, cheese, butter, suet, and casks of lemon juice.

Winthrop declared a day of Thanksgiving. Once again, God had provided for His people.

✝   ✝   ✝

The Puritans had obeyed their call, and God had honored their obedience. From Salem, they moved on to settle Boston and other New England towns. Everywhere they went, they established churches and communities that practiced covenant love. Slowly, God was unfolding the design of His kingdom to come.

CHAPTER
EIGHT

*So, we who are many, are one body in Christ, and
individually members one of another. (Romans 12:5)*

THE PURITAN
WAY

From the discovery by Columbus to
the work of missionaries in the
Southwest to the settlement by the
Pilgrims, the Light of Christ spread
in the New World. Now it was
being carried forth by the Puritans.
From 1630 to 1646, twenty thousand
Puritans came to America. They
sailed across the ocean as obedient ser-
vants to the Lord. They came committed
to God and to one another. They yearned to build communities filled with spiritual wisdom and insight—towns and
cities whose life centered on God's word.

Many people today do not know this about the Puritans.
They think that the Puritans were a somber group of people
who always dressed in black. They believe that the Puritans
had nothing better to do than attend long church services.
They view these settlers as narrow-minded and self-right-
eous.

Were they? What were the Puritans really like?

✝ ✝ ✝

"Don't forget to check the inn, Allen!" the pastor called. "Make sure it's closed during the service today."

"I will, Pastor," the tithingman replied. "I'll also keep an eye on Mr. Tomlins this morning. Last Sunday, he kept closing his eyes. I'll use my staff if I need to. That should keep his eyes open!"

"That will do nicely!" The pastor smiled with a twinkle in his eye.

In Puritan New England, the Sunday morning service usually lasted three to four hours. The church members gathered in the meetinghouse and they paid a tithingman to keep them alert during the teaching. The Puritans realized that sometimes it was difficult to stay awake, but it was important for everyone to hear God's Word. Because they hungered for the Word, the Puritans welcomed long services. They deeply desired a life centered on Christ.

"We must take sin seriously," the pastor preached. "The success of God's New Israel depends on our willingness to lay our sinful natures aside.

"The key to God's plan in our lives is that we remember we are sinners. We must remain humble before Him. We must always remember that we need His mercy and forgiveness at every turn. His blessings will flow from our obedience."

While the pastor spoke, the tithingman quietly walked around the meetinghouse. He strutted about, watching for anyone who might be "resting his eyes." Sure enough, Mr. Tomlins was sleeping comfortably. His head leaned against the wall while his hand grasped the rail. The tithingman quickly pricked the man's hand with the sharp thorn attached to the end of his staff. The man sprang up with such force that he struck his hand against the wall.

"Curse you, woodchuck!" Tomlins loudly exclaimed. He had been dreaming and thought a woodchuck had bitten his hand. When he realized where he was, the embarrassed man sat down and did not fall asleep again!

The heart of the Puritans' lives was their willingness to deal with sin. Sin separated them from God, and the Puritans took it very seriously. They knew that the success of God's kingdom depended on their understanding of sin. The Puritans dealt with it in two ways. They looked at the sin within their own hearts, and they looked at the sins of others. Understanding sin required strict obedience to the Bible and great personal discipline. Understanding sin also required repentance and forgiveness. The Puritans were willing to do it all.

The case of Captain John Underhill was a good example.

"Now, Captain Underhill," the pastor began, "you may speak."

John Underhill stood before the congregation with tears in his eyes. "My sin was adultery. It was a sin against you as well as against God. You were right to cut me off from the church. It's made me realize I was wrong." The captain swallowed hard. "I ask you to forgive me."

The congregation listened. One of the members spoke up. "Brother Underhill, how do we know you've truly repented of your sins?"

Underhill took a deep breath. "Because my heart has changed. I'm asking you to have compassion on me," he said. "I'm truly sorry for what I've done."

The church had excommunicated Captain Underhill. It hoped that he would come to repentance. Excommunication was a severe punishment in the 1600s. The church served as the center of social as well as religious life. Being cut off from it meant being cut off from everything. And Underhill did not want that. He repented, and the congregation forgave him.

At the center of the Puritans' lives was their covenant relationship with God and with one another. This covenant shaped everything they did, and they took it very seriously. The covenant was based on Christ's Great Commandment:

> You shall love the Lord your God with all
> your heart and with all your soul and with
> all your mind. This is the great and foremost
> commandment. And a second is like it, You
> shall love your neighbor as yourself.
> Matthew 22: 37-39

The covenant had two parts: a vertical relationship with Jesus and a horizontal relationship with one another. Both parts must be honored in order for individuals and a community to function properly.

They were family. They had been called into a special relationship. When it came to matters of birth and death, they rejoiced and grieved together. Training children was a sacred responsibility undertaken by both parents and church.

Marriage was a sacred vow, carefully entered only after counsel from other brethren. What happened to one Puritan affected every Puritan. Each of them was part of the big family.

They were also a people who enjoyed life. Frequently, they met to build a house or hold a meeting. Quilting and sewing bees were favorite pastimes for the women. Children would gather together for games and spelling bees.

In 1682, some Puritans assembled to dedicate a new meetinghouse and to install their new pastor. Ministers from churches for miles around were invited as guests. A member of the congregation offered his barn for the dedication dinner.

While the boys swept, the girls hung large green bows and wreaths. They placed benches for the women and set a long table in the middle of the barn floor.

"Anna, you and Roger take the cows to the field," Mrs. Hood directed. "Thomas and I will shoo off the chickens. Rebecca, you and Sarah set the table. It's almost time for Mr. Shepherd and the others to arrive."

Soon the guests arrived. The new pastor, Mr. Shepherd, sat down with the other guests of honor. They enjoyed a feast of meats, puddings, and fruit pies. They discussed the dedication sermon and the new meetinghouse.

Suddenly, a flock of chickens flew into the barn and landed in the rafters. They scattered feathers and dirt all over the table. The guests looked up from their plates in shock.

"Get those birds away!" ordered Mrs. Hood.

The chickens flew out, only to turn around and fly back in.

Mr. Shepherd watched in silence while the birds continued to be a nuisance. Finally, he picked up an apple and threw it at one of them. He hit its legs, causing it to flop down on the table. Gravy and sauces splattered on the diners' faces. Everyone burst into laughter. Mrs. Hood removed the bird, and everyone returned to eating.

The feast continued, but not without more invading roosters and flying apples. Songs and laughter filled the occasion. This was the Puritan way.

Because the Puritans were deeply committed to God, He blessed them frequently. Cotton Mather, a famous Puritan minister, wrote a book entitled *Magnalia*. He described many of God's wondrous miracles in the New World.

One story was about two ships at sea. One sprang a leak when it was more than a thousand miles from shore. Its crew climbed into the longboat, carrying bread and water. By the eighteenth day, they still had ample bread but only enough water to give each man one teaspoon per day. In the meantime, the other ship had run out of food. This ship spied the drifting longboat.

"Captain Scarlet," a seaman cried, "there's a longboat starboard! It's filled with men."

"Aye," the captain replied as he walked to the starboard side. "They're in distress. We'll take them in!"

"But Captain," the first mate said, "we don't have enough food for ourselves. How can we take on more people?"

"These men are in trouble," the captain declared. "God will have to provide for us all."

And God did. Captain Scarlet's ship had plenty of water. The men in the longboat had plenty of food. When the sailors arrived in New England, they spread the word about God's miracle.

God was planting His spiritual vineyard in the colonies with faithful followers. But all of the branches needed to be strong. Before long, He began to prune a few vines from the Bay Colony.

The first such separation involved a man named Roger Williams. Williams was a Puritan minister who did not share the Puritan vision for God's kingdom. He did not believe God would use human beings to set up His kingdom on earth. Williams demanded perfection from his congregation, yet he would not admit his own shortcomings. Puritan leaders tried to reason with him, but he would not listen.

In 1631, Williams finally said farewell to Massachusetts and moved to Rhode Island, where he founded the city of Providence. His work there with the Narraganset Indians spared Rhode Island from a surprise massacre.

God had to prune another branch from the Bay Colony as well. Her name was Anne Hutchinson. Mrs. Hutchinson was a member of John Cotton's church in Boston. She admired Cotton's preaching and often invited women to her home to discuss his sermons. At first, these discussions focused on the sermons. But as time passed, they revolved around Mrs. Hutchinson and her beliefs. Before long, the woman claimed that she alone knew what the Holy Spirit was saying. The church had no choice but to charge her with heresy.

The courtroom was packed. Every minister within two days' ride was there. Even Governor Winthrop attended.

"Mrs. Hutchinson, how do you know it's not Satan who shows you these things?" the judges asked.

"By an immediate voice!" Mrs. Hutchinson shot back with fire in her eyes.

"How?"

"By the voice of God's Spirit to my soul!" she cried. "And He has told me what He's going to do to you! He's going to ruin you and your children—and this whole Colony."

The Court banished Anne Hutchinson, and she moved away. In 1634, she died at the hands of Indians.

God took a third spiritual branch from the vineyard and replanted it in another colony. This branch was led by the Reverend Thomas Hooker, a friend of John Winthrop. Hooker shared Winthrop's vision of God's purpose for New England. He loved the Lord and had a humble spirit. But he differed from his friend in one important area—who should have the right to vote.

One evening the two men sat in Winthrop's parlor in front of a fire.

"Can you be serious?" Winthrop asked. "You mean that every man should be able to vote?" Winthrop got up to warm himself by the fire. "Thomas, how long do you think God would stay in office if the kingdom of God were a democracy? Government by the consent of the governed is one thing, but every man with a vote?"

Hooker took a sip from his cup. "John, where are the checks and balances in the Bay system of government? What happens if your successor happens to be a bad apple? What if he is not dedicated to the Lord? What do we do then?"

Winthrop turned toward his friend. "Thomas, most men don't have the wisdom to elect good leaders. Government is better off in the hands of a few who are dedicated to God's work."

The two men could never agree on this point, but they remained friends. Hooker finally asked permission to move his church to Connecticut.

"I believe that it's God's will for me to go, John," Hooker said. "It will benefit both colonies. We can continue to support one another."

With a heavy heart, Winthrop sadly addressed his old friend. "You have my permission—and my blessing."

Hooker's ideas planted the roots of the future government in Connecticut. Later this government would serve as a model for the other colonies. Thomas Hooker believed that men should voluntarily consent to the same kind of covenant in civil government that formed the Puritan churches. His ideas laid one more stone in the building that would soon become American democracy.

✛ ✛ ✛

The Puritans were a people of God, deeply committed to the Covenant Way of Life. From John Winthrop's arrival in 1630, the Covenant Way developed and advanced as the Puritans built their new lives. God's light was shining as He built His spiritual house. That is, it was shining for a while . . .

CHAPTER
NINE

*Behold, I set before you this day a blessing and a
curse: the blessing, if you obey the commandments
of the Lord your God . . . and the curse, if you do not
obey the commandments of the Lord your God.
(Deuteronomy 11:26-28)*

KING PHILIP'S WAR

The Puritans believed that hard times were over. They had established their towns. They enjoyed comfortable homes and plenty of food. They were at peace with their neighbors, the Indians. By the end of the seventeenth century, things had changed dramatically. Many Puritans were moving west and becoming pioneers. The hardships of their forefathers were only stories of the past. The Puritans were changing. They were forgetting the Covenant Way.

✝ ✝ ✝

The minister could see it coming. Sunday after Sunday he warned the congregation with passages from the Bible.

"Do not forget the Lord your God. Keep His commandments," the pastor preached. "You have plenty to eat. You have nice homes. Your herds are growing, and your wealth is increasing. Beware! It's easy now to forget the Lord."

The pastor studied his congregation. Some of them were listening, but many were gazing out the window. He went on.

"In Deuteronomy 8, God warned the Israelites that He alone gives the power to get wealth. The Bible warns us not to forget the Lord our God, or we will perish."

The pastor sighed. He knew the people were listening only with their ears. Their hearts were far away.

That evening, two Puritan brothers sat on the steps of their front porch, watching the cows in the pasture. The sun cast long shadows across the yard.

"You know, Jonathan, the pastor has a point," said Samuel. "Deuteronomy does warn us about curses against those who forget the Lord."

"Don't be silly," argued Jonathan. "We've heard this sermon before. God's not going to send curses. He's blessing us. Why, look at this farm. Look at our herds."

"That's true," replied Samuel as he chewed on a piece of grass. "We have worked mighty hard to get this far. But maybe we ought to give God more credit."

"God helps those who help themselves, doesn't He?" Jonathan responded. "He's not going to judge us for helping ourselves. Let the preacher worry about the curses. We need to worry about our land and our herds."

The preachers *were* worried. To be sure, God was blessing the Puritans, but He was also sending warning signals. During the summer of 1646, a great army of caterpillars swarmed down on Rhode Island and Massachusetts. The countryside turned brown as the insects ate everything in their path. There were droughts that left the land dry.

Smallpox epidemics broke out, killing many people. Ships were lost at sea.

The ministers knew this meant judgment if the people did not stop and repent. Some people did turn their hearts back to God. When this happened, God gladly returned the blessings. But gradually, most people were shifting their allegiance away from God. Independence and selfishness were claiming their hearts.

Finally, God's patience came to an end.

"Look!" Roger yelled. "There's something out there, on the surface of the pond."

"I see it," Matthew replied. "Look's like a man's hat and a musket."

"I think the ice will hold us," said Dan. "Let's go see what it is."

It was an early winter morning in Middleborough, fifteen miles from Plymouth. The men walked across the frozen pond. Sure enough, they discovered a hat and gun.

"Look at this!" Roger gasped as his mouth dropped open. "It's a face!"

Underneath the ice was a face. Its eyes were staring straight up, and dark hair floated in the water.

The men chopped the body out of the ice with an ax.

"I know who this is!" Roger exclaimed. "It's John Sassamon, the Christian Indian from Nemasket. He must have drowned."

"But Indians don't make mistakes like that," Matthew argued. "Indians don't walk out on a frozen pond and drown."

"You're right, Matthew," Dan added. "He's not bloated with water like he drowned. And he's got that big knot on his forehead."

"And look at this," Roger answered. "His neck's been broken! Someone killed him! But why?"

John Sassamon had been a Christian Indian from the Wampanoag tribe. After graduating from Harvard, he returned to his tribe and became an aide to the chief. This chief was Metacomet, the son of Massasoit. The settlers called him Philip. Sassamon stayed with Philip for a while before moving to the Indian community of Nemasket to preach. This angered Philip. Philip hated Christian Indians. To him, they were traitors.

An eyewitness to Sassamon's murder was found. This Indian had seen the whole thing from the top of a nearby hill. He was close enough to recognize three men, one of whom was a chief lieutenant to Philip.

The trial was set for June. The verdict was quick and sure. The three defendants were sentenced to death by hanging.

Philip was furious. A guilty verdict connected him to the murder, for everyone thought he must have given the order. Philip insisted that the witness was lying, but then a strange thing happened at the hanging. As the trap door beneath the last of the three Indians was sprung, the rope broke. The terrified Indian fell to the ground and chose to talk. He confessed that the three had killed Sassamon.

Philip's anger boiled over. Settlers began to see large bands of armed Indians moving through the countryside. Those settlers who lived far from neighbors had to move to places guarded by fortified houses. Tension filled the air.

Then came the June attack on Isaac Trowbridge and his family. Trowbridge awoke with a start. *What was that?* he wondered.

He jumped up from his bed to look out the window of his house. The morning air in Swansea was cool and clear. The sky was pink and gray in the early dawn. Trowbridge squinted his eyes. He could not see anything.

He heard the noise again! "Something has hit the front door!" he yelled. Trowbridge raced to the door and opened it. His eyes widened in horror when he saw the arrow. Before he could slam the door shut, another arrow sank deep into his chest. Then a third arrow pierced his throat. His oldest son tried to drag his father inside, but an arrow hit him, too.

At that moment, the surrounding woods erupted with Indians. The middle son bolted the door and pushed the table against the front window. The youngest son loaded their father's long-barreled rifle. But all was lost, and the family knew it. Before long, the Indians had killed each of them and set the house on fire.

That day, Indians from Mount Hope burned all the houses in Swansea. When the colonial troops finally arrived, they were horrified at the scene. The main street of the little village was covered with the bodies of men, women, and children. How could human beings have done this?

This happened on June 21, 1675. The next day, the Indians attacked Dartmouth, Taunton, Middleborough, and Sudbury. God had lifted His protective grace. And New England was not prepared for it. Massachusetts declared a day of fasting as reports of more disasters arrived.

"God's wrath is not going to be turned around by one day of repentance," Cotton Mather warned. "He is demanding a complete change in heart. He is telling us to root out the sins within us."

Cotton Mather's father, Increase Mather, joined him. "Listen to the words of Jeremiah," he said, "'Behold, I am bringing a nation against you. . . It is an ancient nation, A nation whose language you do not know . . . They seize bow and spear; They are cruel and have no mercy; Their voice roars like the sea'" (Jeremiah 5:15, 6:23).

At first, the settlers did not take the sermons seriously. But as the attacks grew worse, they began to listen. Yankee self-confidence and independence would not win this war. The settlers needed God.

The fighting became worse. Before long, almost every Indian tribe in New England was wearing war paint and taking scalps. The Indians had decided it was time to push the white man back to the sea. They had nothing to lose. Their backs faced the Hudson River where the hostile Iroquois tribe lived. This was their last chance if they were to live in New England.

But this fighting was more than a war over territory. This was a spiritual battle. God's patience with the colonists had come to an end. He had lifted His divine protection from them. An army of Indians had gone on the warpath—and they were winning!

Yet, God continued to take care of His people by showing them special favor. The siege of Brookfield, Massachusetts, was an example.

The townspeople of Brookfield crowded into the block-house. The men loaded their muskets and fired at the Nipmucks.

"Curtis, you've got to try once more," one of the men pleaded. "We're not going to hold out much longer. There are too many of them."

A nearby window shattered as a flaming arrow crashed through. The women grabbed some blankets to put it out.

"You're right, William," Curtis replied. "Someone has to get to Marlborough."

That night, Curtis opened the door and ran out as the men fired their guns to cover him. He dashed across the opening to a large barrel where he stopped to catch his breath. Curtis crouched down beside the barrel. *If I can just make it to the woods without being seen,* he thought.

After a few moments, Curtis sprang up and headed for the woods. He fell to the ground on his hands and knees. *Oh Lord,* he prayed, *close their eyes to me.* The man crawled through the darkness with sweat pouring down his cheeks. His heart was pounding in his chest. He tried not to make a sound.

Nipmucks are everywhere, and Marlborough is thirty miles away, he thought. *I've got to make it, Lord.*

Meanwhile, the Nipmucks had moved to the barns near the blockhouse. They shot flaming arrows into the roof, but the settlers cut a hole in the roof and put out the flames. The Indians next piled hay against a corner of the house and set it on fire. Some brave settlers rushed outside and threw water on it. The Indians were really angry by this point. They built a torch out of gunpowder and loaded it onto a wagon. Just as they set it in motion, a sudden rain completely drenched the powder. It was no good! The Indians could not use the torch.

Forty-eight hours later, the townspeople were still holding out. Curtis made it to Marlborough. When word reached Major Samuel Willard, he dispatched his troops immediately. Brookfield was saved thanks to God's protective hand.

Crowds poured into the churches. For the first time in a long time, people listened to the sermons with more than their ears. They listened with their hearts. And for the first time in a long time, they got down on their knees to pray. Many churches even renewed their covenants.

These things pleased the Lord, who permitted the circumstances to change. And He used some very unusual people to help—"Praying Indians." These were Christian Indians, who had remained loyal to their Christian brethren. These Indians fought alongside the settlers, and their assistance changed the tide of the war.

The Praying Indians taught the settlers how to fight as Indians do. They knew how to move swiftly through the dense forest and hide in the woods, and they understood how to ambush an enemy. As they demonstrated these tactics to the settlers, changes took place. By the summer of 1676, the settlers could no longer be run away by flaming arrows and battle cries. They were eager to fight, and they were determined to win. With the Lord on their side, they could withstand anything.

It was the summer of 1676. One day, a Wampanoag strolled into the camp of Captain Benjamin Church.

"I must see your captain," the Indian demanded. The soldiers escorted him to Church's tent.

"Captain," the Indian began, "I've come to help you. I can take you to Philip."

"What?" the Captain replied. "Why would you do that?"

"Because Philip murdered my family," he said. "They suggested he make peace, and he became angry. He had them killed. I don't want to be part of his band any longer."

"Where is he?" Church asked.

"He's returned to the Wampanoag settlement at Mount Hope. It's on the peninsula of Bristol Neck in Rhode Island."

In the dead of night, Church moved his men in canoes onto the peninsula and set up an ambush.

"Lieutenant," Church said, "have your troops approach the settlement from here, up north." Church pointed to his map. "Then lie still through the night. We'll form a wide perimeter to the south. When the Indians try to escape, we'll be waiting for them."

The plan went like clockwork. The soldiers attacked at dawn on August 26. They stormed the camp shouting and whooping. The tremendous noise terrified the Wampanoags, who fled straight into Church's forces to the south. Philip was killed and the Indians surrendered.

King Philip's War was over.

✝   ✝   ✝

It had been a hard battle, but the settlers had fought and won. They had turned their hearts back to God. What lay in store for them now?

TEN

"And it shall be in the last days," God says, "that I
will pour forth of My Spirit upon all mankind."
(Acts 2:17)

THE GREAT AWAKENING

The colonial period in America began when Jamestown was settled in 1607. It continued from the settlement of this first colony until the War for Independence in 1775. During this period, the English settled thirteen colonies along the Atlantic coast. The northern colonies were Connecticut, Massachusetts, New Hampshire, and Rhode Island. The middle colonies were New Jersey, New York, Delaware, and Pennsylvania. Georgia, Maryland, North Carolina, South Carolina, and Virginia formed the southern colonies. Following the Pilgrims and Puritans, many religious groups sailed to the colonies to enjoy freedom in their worship.

By the 1700s, the religious zeal of the Puritans had died away. A spiritual slumber had settled over the colonies. Then, in 1734, something happened. The colonists woke up to the calling of God. They began to realize, once again, that God had a plan for their lives. And this changed them into one nation—one nation under God.

✛ ✛ ✛

God chose a pastor in Northampton, Massachusetts, to start the revival. He was Jonathan Edwards. In December 1734, some surprising events took place in his church, and he recorded them in his *Narrative of Surprising Conversions*.

"The Spirit of God began to fall on us in the most amazing way," he wrote. "At first, five or six people were saved. Then, a young woman with a bad reputation met the Lord. News of her conversion spread like lightning around the town."

Edwards continued. "I talked with many people privately and learned how God had spoken to their hearts. By the summer of 1735, Northampton was filled with the presence of God. You could see it in people's faces. You could feel it in the worship services. The love and joy of the Holy Spirit were present in almost every house. Visitors to our town enjoyed God's blessings, too."

What a revival! God was pouring down His Holy Spirit on the townspeople of Northampton. The revival soon moved from Northampton to other towns in Massachusetts. At the same time, it was spreading in the other colonies, too. Men such as William Tennant and Samuel Davies proclaimed the good news of Jesus Christ. They spread it throughout New Jersey, Pennsylvania, and Virginia. David Brainerd even took it to the Indians in the backwoods of some of the northern colonies. But God used a young British evangelist to spread the good news throughout the thirteen colonies. This young man's name was George Whitefield.

In 1737, George Whitefield sailed from England to the colony of Georgia in America. He believed God had called him to preach there. He sat in his cabin on the ship, reading the Bible. Then he stopped, marked his place, and began to pray.

Lord Jesus, I had to be born again, just like Nicodemus. I had to learn that you love me no matter what. I had to trust you like a little child.

Lord, I want to preach this message in America. I want to help the colonists see how much You love each of them. Help me show them that You have a calling on their lives.

Whitefield arrived in Georgia. He discovered a great hunger for the Word of God. Soon, he was preaching to crowds of people.

After a few months, Whitefield returned to England to raise money for an orphanage in Georgia. England was experiencing a revival, too. Whitefield spoke in the towns of Bristol and Gloucestor to anyone who would listen. He explained sin and the need for forgiveness. He talked about the need to be born again. And he told them about the Savior. But not everyone wanted to listen. Whitefield found pulpits closed to him by jealous preachers.

Whitefield sat in the home of his two friends from Oxford University, John and Charles Wesley. George sat in a big armchair while John stood beside his desk. Charles rested on the cream-colored sofa.

"Maybe God doesn't want you to preach in those churches, George. Maybe He wants you to do something else. The preachers here are jealous. That's why they won't let you in."

John Wesley arranged the papers on his desk as he spoke.

"You remember how people laughed at us?" Charles asked. "They called us 'Methodists' because we chose to worship in a special way. People here are hungry for the Word of God just as they are in the colonies."

Whitefield stood up and walked over to the fireplace. "I can only think of one way to get the Word out," he announced, "but no one has ever tried it."

"What is it?" John asked.

"To go out in the open air and preach as Jesus used to do."

"That's a great idea, George!" Charles exclaimed. "Think of how many people we could reach. And you have such a strong, deep voice. People could hear you across a field!"

"It could work," John added thoughtfully. "Yes, I think that just might work. Maybe this is what God wants us to do."

"All right, then. Let's do it!" And the three men agreed.

Whitefield decided to preach to the coal miners on the outskirts of Bristol. He knew they were a mean and nasty bunch, but they needed a Savior just as much as anyone. The evangelist stood on a hill near the exit of the mines, waiting for the men to come out. It was winter, and the air was cold and damp. The setting sun cast long shadows toward the mines. Soon the miners began drifting out, and Whitefield started preaching.

"Jesus Christ died for you," he called. "He loves you that much. He gave his life on the cross to pay for your sins. His only thought was for you. He suffered and died that you might receive everlasting life."

A few miners stopped to listen. Whitefield went on. Before long, several hundred men were standing on the hill listening to the message. Whitefield noticed pale streaks running down their black, grimy faces. An old man wiped away tears with his dirty sleeve. A huge miner with bulging muscles blew his nose. Whitefield knew the Spirit of God was moving on their hearts.

The ministers in Bristol were not happy about Whitefield's preaching, but he did not stop. The following Sunday, ten thousand people gathered to hear him. By the third week in March 1739, more than double that number came out to hear him. Revival swept the English Midlands.

The young evangelist traveled all over England that summer. By the time he sailed back to America in August, he had preached to more people than any one man alive. He was, in fact, becoming one of the greatest evangelists of the century.

But what happened in England was minor in comparison to what was about to happen in America. Whitefield was anxious to return because he believed God had a special message for the colonies. He hoped that his preaching would help unite the thirteen colonies scattered along the eastern coast. He believed that God wanted them to become one nation under Him.

On his first night in Philadelphia, Whitefield stood on the steps of the courthouse. People jammed the streets to hear the "boy preacher" from England. Whitefield began to preach.

"Father Abraham," Whitefield asked, "who do you have there in heaven? Any Episcopalians?"

"No!" Whitefield answered his own question.

"Do you have any Presbyterians?" he asked.

"No!"

"Are there any Methodists?"

"No! No! No!" Whitefield's deep voice got louder as he raised his arms in the air. "Well then, Father Abraham, who is with you?"

"There are only Christians here—followers of the Lord Jesus."

"Oh!" Whitefield responded. "Then let us forget that we come from different colonies. Let us forget that we go to different churches. As Christians, we are all part of one big family—the family of God."

Standing in the crowd was a man named Benjamin Franklin. Franklin was already famous throughout the colonies as a scientist, a philosopher, and a publisher. But he was not a man of God. He was an agnostic who believed that questions about God could not be answered. Franklin liked to experiment, so he backed down Market Street while Whitefield was talking.

"I'm going to see just how far this young man's voice can travel," Franklin muttered.

He walked until he could not hear the preacher. *My, my, he* said to himself, *this is quite a distance. My guess is that this young fellow could preach to thirty thousand people if he were out in an open field!*

Later, Franklin described the change in the city of Philadelphia. "People everywhere are becoming religious," he wrote. "You can't walk down the street without hearing psalms being sung. People's manners are improving too. Philadelphia is a different place."

Whitefield traveled up and down the east coast. He preached in Boston and Providence. He journeyed to Baltimore and New Haven. He went south to places like

Charleston and Savannah. He rode into the frontier on horseback and in a canoe. Everywhere he went, crowds of people swarmed to hear him.

One day, Whitefield suddenly decided to speak in Middletown, Connecticut. Riders galloped ahead to spread the word. "The man who preaches like the apostles of old is coming!" they yelled. Farmers dropped their hoes and left their plows. They mounted their horses and thundered down the dirt road toward Middletown. When the evangelist arrived, several thousand horses had been tethered in long lines behind a vast crowd of dust-covered farmers. It looked as if an entire cavalry division had dismounted and was awaiting him!

To win America for God, Whitefield had to win New England, but New England had grown cold to the things of God. Whitefield blamed the clergy. "The clergy lack life," he wrote. "Their sermons are dead. They do not know the risen Christ in their hearts. They practice religion as the Pharisees used to do, and their Christianity has lost its power." Whitefield realized that the church leadership must experience revival, too. Some of the pastors did not want to hear this, but others did. And many of these men changed.

Preaching sometimes two and three times a day, George Whitefield gave more than eighteen thousand sermons between 1736 and 1770. By then, the colonies' relationship with England was breaking down. Whitefield's last sermon in Boston was delivered five months after the Boston Massacre. This was one of the early signs of the trouble to come. British troops had fired on angry colonists, killing five of them. Colonial resentment was growing stronger.

Whitefield's message became even more important.

On a Saturday afternoon in September, Whitefield delivered the final sermon of his life in Exeter, New Hampshire. At first, he had difficulty talking, so he paused for a few moments. "I'll wait for God's help," he said. "I know He's going to let me speak one last time."

Whitefield did speak. His voice rose, becoming loud and clear, and he preached for two hours.

Finally he proclaimed, "I'm going to be with Jesus. I have lived to preach for Him. Now I shall die and be with Him. My body is failing, but my spirit is growing stronger."

The next morning, George Whitefield went to be with the Lord.

Through the preaching of George Whitefield, God brought the thirteen colonies together. It was not long before many people realized what was happening. The Holy Spirit was speaking, through this evangelist, to the hearts of people everywhere. It did not matter in what colony a person lived. The Spirit could still touch that person's heart.

Whitefield spread the word about God's love and salvation through Jesus Christ. He carried it to rich and poor alike. He revealed it to free men and to slaves, to the educated and the uneducated. Over and over, Americans everywhere received the message that all men are equal and precious in the sight of God.

Gradually, the colonists realized they were part of a big family. They understood that God had a special plan for this family. He wanted it to proclaim the true message of Jesus. He wanted it to be a light in the darkness. And He wanted this family to become the living example of the Covenant

Way. The colonists had experienced a Great Awakening.

✞   ✞   ✞

God was setting another spiritual stone in the foundation of the nation. The Pilgrims had signed the Mayflower Compact. The Puritans had brought the Covenant Way. Now, the colonies were uniting through the Spirit of the One True God. Very soon, the principles they were learning would be written down by a new generation of people who called themselves "Americans."

CHAPTER
ELEVEN

*It was for freedom that Christ set us free; therefore,
keep standing firm and do not be subject to a yoke of
slavery. (Galatians 5:1)*

"NO KING
BUT KING JESUS!"

One nation under God—this was the spiritual result of the Great Awakening. Colonial Americans learned some important lessons during that time. They realized that God was their Heavenly Father and they could depend on Him. They also realized that they were all brothers and sisters in Christ. The nation was waking up.

This was a new event in the history of man. God had never uprooted a body of Christians and planted them in a new land. But He did in colonial America. He had never let such a group create a civil government led by the Holy Spirit. But He did in colonial America.

In 1775, the colonists revolted against England. Why did they want to throw off the yoke of Britain? Was it in God's will for them to rebel against their mother country? What happens when a ruler makes it impossible for his subjects to follow the will of God?

✛ ✛ ✛

It was a cold day in January 1684. Increase Mather hurried down the cobblestone street toward Boston's Old South Meetinghouse. A cold wind was blowing, and Mather clutched his papers tightly.

A few minutes later, he arrived. Inside, a huge crowd jammed the meetinghouse. They had assembled to vote on Boston's response to a declaration made by King Charles. Mather walked up to the pulpit and placed his papers on the stand. As he looked out over the large crowd, his mind wandered back to the events which had brought them to this point.

After the founding of Plymouth, English settlers had flocked to the New World. Unlike the French and Spanish, they did not come to seek riches. They came to begin a new life. They built cabins and farms. They established villages and towns. They organized churches and set up schools. And they set up local governments to govern their affairs.

Mather thought about his grandfathers, John Cotton and Richard Mather. He thought about the hopes and dreams they had shared with him. "God has sent us to America," they had said, "and He has a plan for us. We are to be like a city set on a hill. We are to shine His Light into a world of darkness."

Mather thought about England's policies with her colonies. For more than a century, Parliament had allowed the colonies to run themselves. Yet the English Parliament had the power to rule over the colonies, and the colonists had to obey English law.

Recently, England had started passing some very strict laws in regard to the colonies. In 1651 and 1663, Parliament enacted the Navigation Acts. These allowed the colonies to trade only with England. Colonial merchants could no longer trade with other merchants.

King Charles then ordered Massachusetts to swear allegiance to the Crown and to let the Episcopal Church set up churches in the colony. And he ordered the colony to change some of its voting requirements.

Massachusetts said *no*. Charles then demanded the return of their charter. He planned to make them a royal colony. The Bay Colony was in trouble. How could it stand up to the greatest military power on earth?

Increase Mather stood in the pulpit and delivered his message.

"The king has demanded that we give up our charter," he said. "Doing this will clash with the very reasons our forefathers came to New England! They came for religious freedom. They came for political freedom. King Charles decrees that we give up these freedoms.

"If we resist," he continued, "we'll face great suffering. But can we give away our inheritance? Which should we choose—to fall into the hands of man or the hand of God? I say we must choose God!

"To give up our charter would be a sin against God!" he proclaimed. "Who of us would dare to sin against God? We must stand on God's side at all cost!"

As Mather finished, he saw tears running down people's faces. When the vote was taken, it was unanimous not to submit. Boston had taken a strong stand against the king of England. Soon other towns in Massachusetts did the same.

Charles II was furious. He determined to send Colonel Percy Kirk and five thousand troops to make Massachusetts obey. Word of "Bloody Kirk's" coming reached Mather in February of 1685. The minister shut himself in his study to pray.

O Lord, we've put ourselves in Your merciful hands, he prayed. *We're like Daniel, who wanted to follow You. Then King Darius demanded that everyone pray only to the king. Daniel knew this would mean disobeying You. Daniel could not disobey You, so he disobeyed the king. When Darius sent him to the lion's den, You saved him. Lord, we need You to save us now, too.*

God spoke to Mather's heart that day and assured him the colony would be safe. Sure enough, two months later, word arrived that Charles II had died. Colonel Kirk would not be coming.

The new king of England, James II, did not send Kirk, but he did send Sir Edmund Andros. And Andros sought to put down any resistance in the colonies. First, he ordered that Episcopal services be held in the Old South Meetinghouse. (The Episcopal Church was the same as the Church of England.) This would force the colonists to worship in the Church of England again. Next, he tried to take away all their charters.

"Hand over your charter!" he demanded one night at the meetinghouse in Hartford. "You Connecticut people must bow down to the king!"

The treasured document lay on a table in a room filled with candles. All of a sudden, the candles went out! There was a great commotion.

"Get that document!" Andros ordered. "Don't let them have it!"

It was too late. When the candles were lit, the charter was gone. Someone had hidden it in the hollow trunk of an old oak tree. Andros never found it.

In 1689, William and Mary took over the throne of England. Peace returned to the colonies until George III became king in 1760.

At that time, England was fighting a war with France. When it was over, England held a great deal of France's territory in the New World. This pleased George III because he wanted to keep the French out of North America and to protect his interests. But there were problems: The war had been expensive and had left England in debt. King George decided the colonies should pay for the British troops he sent to America. Since the colonies had no representatives in Parliament, they could not object. Parliament began passing tax laws.

First came the Molasses Act of 1733. This act required a three cent tax on each gallon of molasses that was not purchased from the British West Indies. This act hurt many merchants in the northern colonies. George III next brought back the Navigation Acts. He sent customs officials to collect the taxes. These officials were greedy and kept much of the money for themselves.

The Stamp Act of 1765 required the colonists to pay for British stamps. The stamps were expensive and the colonists had to put them on all printed matter from marriage certificates to newspapers. The colonists protested, and Parliament finally repealed it.

But the tax laws did not end there. In 1767, Parliament passed more. Next were the Townshend Acts that forced the colonies to pay taxes on glass, paint, paper, lead, and tea. George III was proving to be a selfish, conceited monarch who wanted to ruin the colonies. He was not raising money to pay for troops in America. He was raising money to pay for England's adventures around the world!

By now the mood in America was ugly and Patriots began to support resistance. They formed Committees of Correspondence which sent letters throughout the colonies. These letters told everyone what was happening. And these Committees became very important to the resistance effort.

In Boston, Jonathan Mayhew spoke out in favor of resistance. "When our officials rob and ruin us, they're nothing but pirates. The king is bound by oath to uphold our legal rights. As soon as he sets himself above the law, he becomes a tyrant. He is no longer a king, and his subjects no longer have to obey him."

A lawyer in New York named William Livingston wrote, "Courage, Americans . . . The land we possess is God's gift to us. Soon, we will be writing an American Constitution."

Ministers across the land supported resistance, too. Many of these ministers had lived through the Great Awakening. They wanted to heed God's call as well. "Where the Spirit of the Lord is, there is liberty," they preached. "When a ruler opposes God's will, his subjects cannot follow God's will. We must stand fast. We must not submit to a yoke of slavery.

"We don't want to rebel. We want peace, and we must work toward peace. But, if resistance is the only way, then we must resist."

In 1769, England withdrew all of the Townshend Acts, except the one on tea. In 1773, Parliament passed the Tea Act because the colonists had refused to buy British tea. This act helped the British East India Tea Company. It permitted the Company to sell tea directly to the colonists without selling to a colonial company first. It could sell its tea for less than any of the American companies could sell theirs.

The colonists were furious. The Committees of Correspondence dispatched urgent letters. "Don't let the Company unload its tea," they said. "Stop them from selling the tea!"

And in Boston, the colonists did just that.

It was a chilly night in December 1773, when Benjamin gazed out his bedroom window. The moonlight beamed on the water of the harbor outside his window. He could see the ships docked there. He could hear the waves against the wharf.

My parents were upset tonight, he thought. *They think something big is going to happen. I wonder what it could be.*

Just then, Benjamin noticed shadows moving toward the wharf. He squinted his eyes. *What's that?* he wondered. *Why, it's Indians! No, it's colonists dressed like Indians!* Benjamin watched the men board one of the ships owned by the East India Tea Company.

"They're dumping tea into the water!" he exclaimed, with his eyebrows raised high.

The men did not stop until they had dumped all the tea into the harbor. Benjamin watched them leave. He knew this signaled trouble.

And it did. As soon as George III received word, he demanded that the men be found. But no one could find them! George decided to punish the entire city by closing the port. This would also be a warning to the other colonies. "They'll not get away with this!" he declared.

By now, the truth was becoming clear. If the king could close the richest port in the colonies, he could close any port in the colonies. If he could ruin their tea companies, he could ruin all colonial merchants.

Their anger erupted. Colonists everywhere joined together to help Boston in her hour of need. Towns in North and South Carolina donated barrels of rice. People in Connecticut gave sheep. A Virginian named George Washington promised money. Maryland and Virginia sent aid, too. The Boston Tea Party had united the colonists in their cry for freedom.

The Committees of Correspondence warned the colonists, "If England can do this to Boston, she can do this to any of us. George III has become a tyrant. We have no king . . . no king but King Jesus!"

In August 1774, William Prescott posted a letter to Boston, "God has placed you where you must stand the first shock. We are all in the same boat. We must sink or swim together. Our forefathers died that we might be free. Let us all be of one heart. Let us stand fast in the freedom Christ has given us."

In October 1774, Massachusetts held a Provisional Congress. Its president, John Hancock, declared: "We must humble ourselves before Almighty God. We must ask Him if we are wrong in some way. We must pray for a peaceful settlement to our differences."

The Congress wrote to Massachusetts Bay. "If God does not will peace, then we must resist. It becomes our Christian duty to resist. Continue steadfast, dear brothers. Remember that your dependence is on God. Defend those rights which heaven gave, and no man can take!"

It was now the dawn of 1775. On March 23, Patrick Henry addressed the Virginia House of Burgesses.

"There is no longer room for hope. If we wish to be free, we must fight! An appeal to arms and to the God of Hosts is all that is left us!

"We are not weak. We shall not fight alone. God presides over the destinies of nations, and will raise up friends to help us. I do not know what course others may take, but as for me, give me liberty or give me death!"

CHAPTER
TWELVE

There is an appointed time for everything. And there is a time for every event under heaven . . . A time for war, and a time for peace.

(Ecclesiastes 3:1, 8)

WAR!

 Resistance in the colonies was growing and England wanted to crush it. King George appointed General Thomas Gage as governor of Massachusetts. General Gage was also the commander of the British forces in America. Gage marched his troops to Boston. In February 1775, Parliament declared that the colony of Massachusetts was in a state of rebellion. British soldiers could now shoot the rebels.

The Bible teaches that God honors obedience with His blessing. He does not honor disobedience. Did He honor the colonists who sought independence? Did He favor their cause? The answer lies hidden in the battles just ahead.

✝ ✝ ✝

"To arms, to arms!" the rider shouted. "The war's begun! They're heading for Concord!" Paul Revere slowed his horse as he approached Lexington, Massachusetts. He had galloped from Boston to sound the alarm. He shouted again and then sped off to warn the others.

It was early dawn on April 19, 1775. Men rushed from their houses. They could be ready in a minute's notice. It was time to fight.

"Stand your ground!" Captain John Parker called to the Minutemen. "Don't fire unless fired upon. If they want war, let it begin here!"

Jonas Parker, the captain's first cousin, rammed a musket ball down the three-foot-long barrel of his musket. Then he put his hat on the ground and filled it with more balls. *I won't run from these Redcoats and their bright jackets*, he thought to himself. On his left, Isaac Muzzey stood at an open keg of gunpowder. Muzzey noticed that Jonathan Harrington was filling his powder horn. Harrington's wife watched them from the upstairs window of their house on the green.

Gage thinks he's going to outsmart us, Muzzey thought. *He thinks he's going to capture all the arms and gunpowder stored in Concord. But he'll have to get by us first!*

The early morning light shone through the shade trees on the green. The sky was clear. All was quiet. Suddenly, the church bell clanged.

"Here they come!" someone cried. The men faced the east corner of the green. They saw the first ranks of a column of British soldiers—several hundred soldiers! Captain Parker quickly realized what he must do.

"Scatter!" he commanded. "There are too many of them! Don't fire. Scatter into the countryside." Parker knew that his few men could not win against so many. Instead of fighting at Lexington, they would beat the British to Concord and join the other Minutemen forces there.

Parker's men turned to retreat. The Redcoats broke ranks and charged across the lawn. Confusion engulfed the green.

Major John Pitcairn, the British commander, yelled out, "Soldiers, don't fire! Keep your ranks! Form and surround them!" The major turned toward the Minutemen and shouted, "Throw down your arms! We won't harm you."

But shots were fired. A young British officer had ordered a volley, and the British militia all discharged their guns at the same time. The Minutemen abruptly halted as smoke covered the green. The British troops quickly formed back into lines and loaded their muskets for a second volley.

"Throw down your arms!" a British officer on horseback called out. "Why don't you rebels lay down your arms?"

This time the Minutemen discharged their muskets. A British officer pointed his sword at the colonists and shouted, "Fire! Fire!" His soldiers fired the second volley that tore into the Minutemen. Jonas Parker fell to the ground, badly wounded. He later died. Isaac Muzzey and Jonathan Harrington were killed. In all, the British killed eight Minutemen and wounded ten.

Some of the British chased the Patriots into the woods. The rest marched down the road toward Concord. Their fifes and drums could be heard in the distance. Quiet returned to the green.

The Battle of Lexington lasted less than fifteen minutes, but it marked the beginning of the War of Independence.

Seven hundred British regulars reached Concord late that morning. By the time they got there, the powder, cannon, and weapons had all been removed and hidden. The main body of Redcoats stayed in Concord while search parties went in different directions to look for Minutemen.

The largest group of soldiers marched up the road toward the North Bridge and over the Concord River just north of town. A squad of one hundred men stayed behind to guard the bridge. What the British did not realize was that the colonial volunteers were ready for them. Every farmer for miles around had answered Revere's call. A Patriot column now shadowed the search party. As soon as the larger group of Redcoats left, the Minutemen filed down toward the British squad at the bridge.

"Pull back!" a British officer commanded. "Pull back!"

The British fired. An officer ordered a volley, which cut down several Minutemen.

"Fire!" an American officer yelled. The Minutemen fired back.

The British soldiers were shocked. This was not like Lexington! These Minutemen were not running away. They were standing their ground and firing back. And they could shoot!

The first British squad knelt to reload. The second took aim behind them.

"George," said one British soldier looking behind him, "where's the third squad?"

George looked over his shoulder quickly and then screamed, "Scatter!"

The third squad of British soldiers had run away from the bridge. Immediately, the rest of them retreated and headed back to Concord. The British decided they had better return to Charlestown quickly, and they began their march.

But the Minutemen were ready once again. All along the way, they stalked the marching British column, ambushing them from the woods.

"Over here, Thomas!" Ben pointed to a large ditch. "We can fire from here."

"James, you and John take cover by that stone wall up the road," the captain ordered. "Shoot from there!"

The march was a nightmare for the British. Minutemen seemed to be everywhere. The Redcoats could not fight a battle when they could not even see their enemy! They were tired from fighting and marching. And by the time they reached Lexington, they were almost out of ammunition. They could not take much more.

Just then the soldiers heard the sound of bagpipes.

"Captain, it's General Percy!" a British lieutenant yelled. "He's come with help!"

Sure enough, Percy had arrived with a thousand fresh men and two cannons. The British made it back to Charlestown.

But the Americans celebrated a victory. They had done it! They had stood up to the greatest military power on earth.

Ministers everywhere reminded the Patriots whom they should thank. "As long as we keep our hearts right, God will shower His blessings on us," they preached. "We cannot take pride in our own strength. It is the God of heaven and earth whom we must thank."

The Reverend Samuel Langdon proclaimed, "If God is for us, who can be against us? Let the Lord be our refuge and our strength."

In New Haven, Connecticut, a young captain named Benedict Arnold marched his men to Massachusetts.

"I think I can take Fort Ticonderoga from the British," he told the Massachusetts Provincial Congress. "It's located on the southern end of Lake Champlain. If we take it, we'll command the waterway from New York City to Montreal. And we'll stop the British from coming down from Montreal."

The members of Congress listened. Arnold continued. "We can use the fort's cannon to fight in Boston. Canada might join us in our fight against the British."

The Provincial Congress agreed with Arnold and made him a colonel. He departed for Canada immediately. Colonel Ethan Allen and his Green Mountain Boys from Vermont joined forces with Arnold on May 9, 1775.

The men crept forward through the gray fog of early morning. They spotted the fort just ahead.

"Look there." Allen whispered. "The gate is open. Let's take it!"

The men rushed in. A sentry raised his musket and aimed at Allen, but the gun did not fire. A few Redcoats appeared, but the Americans took them prisoner. Allen stormed up the stairs to the commander's headquarters and banged on the door.

"Captain Delaplace, deliver this fort instantly!" Allen demanded.

"By what authority?" Delaplace replied.

"In the name of the great Jehovah and the Continental Congress!" Allen roared.

Delaplace ordered his forty men to lay down their arms. God had given the Americans the gateway to New York.

On June 15, Colonel William Prescott and his men learned that Gage planned to occupy the Charlestown Neck and Dorchester peninsulas. These were two peninsulas located to the north and south of Boston. The British already held Boston and its harbor. The Americans knew they had to move fast.

"O Lord, we seek Your divine protection this day," Reverend Langdon prayed as the men bowed their heads. "We place ourselves in Your hands as we do what must be done. Have mercy on us."

Prescott and his troops moved onto Charlestown Neck. They began to fortify Breed's Hill, one of the two hills located on the peninsula. It was closer to Boston than the other hill, known as Bunker Hill. The Patriots worked through the night of June 16. They dug a redoubt, which was a fortification on the hill.

By morning, General Gage had learned the colonial forces were there. He ordered an attack.

"Open fire!" he commanded his ships in the harbor. "We're going to settle some old scores today. We're going to watch Yankee Doodle run!"

Gage committed one-third of his entire force to the operation. This would be an important victory. The winner would hold the entire area. Gage appointed General William Howe as field commander.

Howe loaded his forces onto small boats to cross over to Charlestown Neck. On reaching shore, the Redcoats formed two lines. Howe himself led the charge.

"I don't expect any one of you to go any farther than I'm willing to go myself!" With that, Howe pulled out his sword and started up the long hill.

The climb was not easy. Drums beat out the call to advance. Behind Howe marched two line of Redcoats. Their ranks were straight and even. Their eyes looked straight ahead. But something was wrong. Where was the enemy? What were they waiting for?

They were waiting for the command to fire. "Don't fire until you see the whites of their eyes!" Prescott ordered. At last he yelled. "Fire!" The Americans blasted the enemy's lines at close range with musket fire. The British fell back.

Howe quickly got his men back into position. The British began to advance up the hill again. This time, Prescott let them come even closer than before. When they were less than ninety feet away, he ordered his men to fire again. The entire British front rank was destroyed. The Redcoats broke rank and ran down the hill to the boats.

Howe was not going to give up. He changed his tactics. This time, he directed his men to charge the redoubt with bayonets. Once again, Prescott waited to give the order until the British were at close range. But this time the Americans did not have enough ammunition. Redcoats poured over the wall.

"If you have a bayonet, meet them!" Prescott ordered. "The rest of you retreat to the rear of the redoubt. Then take aim!"

The Americans stayed in position as long as they could. Some used their muskets as clubs, but they could not hold the British back. Colonel Prescott finally ordered a retreat.

Strangely, Howe did not pursue Prescott and his men. He easily could have taken Cambridge, which was only two miles away. And he could have taken thousands of patriot prisoners. But he chose to stay where he was. This was just the first of many golden opportunities the British would miss during the war.

The British had won the battle of Bunker Hill. But the victory cost them dearly. Nearly half of their 2,200 soldiers were killed or wounded. The Americans lost only 441 men out of the 3,000 who fought.

Amos Farnsworth, a corporal in the Massachusetts militia, wrote about that day in his diary:

> "Oh, the goodness of God in preserving my life,
> although they fell on my right hand and on my
> left! O may this act of deliverance of thine,
> O God, lead me never to distrust thee . . ."

✝   ✝   ✝

The Americans had resorted to arms, and God seemed to be blessing their cause. But their militia was not yet strong enough. The colonists needed an intelligent, skillful military leader. As always, God had just the man in mind. His name was George Washington.

CHAPTER
THIRTEEN

Do not fear or be dismayed because of this great
multitude, for the battle is not yours but God's.
(2 Chronicles 20:15)

THE BIRTH OF
A NATION

It was a warm morning in June 1775. The tall, blue-eyed Virginian walked toward his horse. The man looked handsome in his new general's uniform of cream-colored breeches and a blue coat. A band played as people jammed the Philadelphia street in front of him.

The general felt embarrassed by all the fuss. He was quiet and gentle by nature, not used to all this attention. But these people wanted to wish him well, and this blessed him. The general reached his horse and mounted. He must be going now. His country had called him into service. God had laid an important task at his feet.

Who was this great man? He was George Washington, the man God chose to help America in her greatest hour of need.

✝ ✝ ✝

One week later, General Washington reached Cambridge, Massachusetts. Thirteen thousand American troops were camped around Boston. They were volunteers who had come from different colonies to fight. They carried their own weapons and knew how to use them. They were farmers and townspeople who had answered the call to arms.

But Washington knew they were not yet soldiers. Most of them had never had any military training. The general's first task was to get his army into shape.

Every morning after prayers, Washington issued new orders such as these:

> The General expects his officers to attend all functions, dressed in correct uniform.

> The General insists on proper military behavior at all times.

> All officers will stop using bad language.

> All men will attend Church services, carrying their arms and ammunition with them.

Washington organized his staff and replaced officers who could not do the job. He ordered training exercises to teach the men the proper way to march and drill. Soldiers who disobeyed were punished. Slowly, the Continental Army began to take shape.

The man chosen to lead this army was more than just a general. He was a man of God. Washington made no secret of his Christian faith. He would ride among his army, directing the soldiers to fear God and to practice Christian virtues. He respected God's word and maintained a daily prayer life.

After the Continental Congress appointed him, Washington quickly realized how much they would need the Lord on their side. Congress had little power to make or enforce laws. The army badly needed ammunition and supplies. But Congress could only raise money when the colonies agreed. And getting the colonies to agree was difficult. Clearly, General Washington would have to rely on divine guidance for this assignment.

As Washington prepared his troops, the Continental Congress approved Ethan Allen and Benedict Arnold's plan to attack Canada. The Congress hoped to stop the British from attacking from the north. Two separate armies advanced toward Quebec, the main British fortress on the Saint Lawrence River.

Colonel Richard Montgomery left Fort Ticonderoga with one army and proceeded toward Montreal. Sickness and bad weather slowed them down, and they did not reach Montreal until late fall. Montgomery captured Montreal and moved on.

Benedict Arnold led the second army along the Kennebec River in Maine into the Maine wilderness. Tragedy lay ahead. First, their riverboats leaked, ruining much of their ammunition and supplies. Then vicious, icy rapids damaged the boats even more. On October 18, 1775, the men slaughtered their two remaining oxen for meat. Over the next four days, a driving rain raised the river ten feet. More boats and supplies were lost. By October 25, the rain had turned to snow and brought the army to a halt. Some men ate candles to stay alive.

"We wandered through the swamps, cold and wet," the army doctor wrote. "We were lost. We were men without hope. We died from hunger and exhaustion."

For three unbelievable days and nights, the men stumbled through the frozen Maine wilderness with nothing to eat. Only six hundred and fifty men survived to arrive in Quebec.

Montgomery's forces joined them on December 2. The Americans had very few men and very little ammunition. They had to act fast.

"We'll wait for a stormy night," Montgomery told Arnold, "and attack from two different directions. I'll take one group and you take the other."

The attack failed. Montgomery was killed, and Arnold was wounded. With the British forces in pursuit, the Patriots retreated. Gradually they fell back to Fort Ticonderoga.

Why did so many things go wrong with the Canadian Campaign? Perhaps God did not want Canada to become part of America. Perhaps the Americans had stepped outside His will. Whatever the reason, the Continental Congress called for a day of fasting and prayer on May 17, 1775. It was time to seek the Lord and ask His forgiveness.

Washington met with his officers. The soldiers drilled just outside the tent. It was November 1775, and the weather in Massachusetts was turning cold. This caused concern.

"Sir, we've got to drive the British out of Boston soon," a major general said. "Winter is upon us."

"How are we going to do it?" another asked. "We have no ammunition or cannons. We can't attack without cannons."

The general sat quietly at his table, listening to the discussion. He had been praying about this, but God had not revealed an answer.

"If we only had a dozen mortars," one officer wished, "or a dozen twelve-pounders. If we only had a dozen anything!"

The situation looked hopeless.

"Wait a minute. What about Ticonderoga?" The officers looked at the colonel who spoke. "Arnold and Allen captured cannon at the fort. Arnold said he'd transport the artillery back to Boston."

"But that was in April when the roads were dry," a brigadier countered. "It's winter now. The roads are muddy and icy. We could never get the guns across the mountains."

Washington stood up and walked around to the front of the table. He leaned against it and crossed his arms.

"Gentlemen," he said, "I sense the hand of God here. Colonel Knox, this is a job for you. What do you say?"

"I can do it, sir," Henry Knox answered.

Knox kept his promise. On the following January 18, over fifty pieces of artillery arrived in Cambridge on sleds!

"Gentlemen," Washington said to his officers, "I've decided to attack. We'll fortify Dorchester Heights, just south of Boston."

"Sir," one of them argued, "we still don't have enough gunpowder. And the ground is frozen. How can we dig a fortification? The British will blow us off the hill!"

"The Almighty will make a way," the general replied.

And He did. A young engineer, who happened to visit one of Washington's generals, spied a book on field engineering. He found a picture of a piece of French equipment called a chandelier. This was a section of wood which held fascines, which were large bundles of sticks. The engineer rushed to tell General Washington.

"General," he said excitedly, "if we construct these chandeliers, we can form a barrier against the British. It'll be as good as a trench!"

"I see," the General replied. "We'll do it. But we'll add something extra. We'll attach barrels of stones to the front of each chandelier. When the British advance, we'll knock the barrels loose. They'll roll down the hill right into the Redcoat lines! I'll have Colonel Knox draw up the plans."

On the night of March 4, construction began. A ground mist covered their work at the base of the hill. The British could not see a thing. An inland breeze carried any noise away from British ears. Once the pieces were fastened, the men loaded them onto large wagons. Horses trudged up the hill, pulling the wagons. At the top of the hill, a clear moonlit night helped the Patriots see what they were doing. God was clearly on their side.

At dawn, the British discovered American cannons pointing straight at them from Dorchester Heights across the inlet! They could not believe it. General Howe called a council of war.

"We'll attack," Howe ordered. "Have two forces ready to go over with the next tide."

The British waited for the tide. But a huge storm blew up. It continued all night, and the British could not strike. By morning, Howe had concluded it was too late. He decided to withdraw. Two weeks later, he moved his troops to New York. Boston now belonged to the Americans.

General Washington recognized the hand of God. Knox had transported the cannons by sled from Fort Ticonderoga. The young engineer had discovered the book on chandeliers. Even the changing weather had assisted them. Not a single life was lost. It was truly a miracle.

On entering Boston, the Americans encountered a terrible truth. The British had no respect for the house of God. They had burned the pulpit and pews in the Old South Church for fuel. They had trained horses in the sanctuary and set up a liquor store in the balcony. Altogether, the British would demolish fifty churches throughout the colonies during the war. The Americans realized that their battle with Britain was really a spiritual battle.

When Congress met in the spring of 1776, it faced a tough question. Should the colonies remain under British authority? The Loyalists said yes. They hoped the king would grant peace. The Patriots said *no*. They saw the king as a hardhearted pharaoh. America was divided.

England was divided, too. Not everyone agreed with King George and the Parliament. Some supported the American cause and would not serve in the armed forces. The king had to hire German mercenaries.

In May 1776, towns across Massachusetts voted in favor of independence. On May 15, the colony of Virginia voted for independence. Yet, the delegates to Congress were still divided. In June 1776, Richard Henry Lee of Virginia formally proposed that Congress declare independence. "These united Colonies are, and of right ought to be, free and independent States," he said. John Adams seconded the proposal.

Congress now had to vote on the proposal. Delegates from the middle colonies asked for time to return home and talk with their people. Congress adjourned for three weeks.

In the meantime, Congress appointed a committee of five men to draft a declaration. Thomas Jefferson prepared the draft:

> *We hold these truths to be self-evident, that all*
> *Men are created equal . . . We, therefore, the repre-*
> *sentatives of the United States of America . . .*
> *appealing to the Supreme Judge of the World . . . do*
> *. . . Publish and Declare, That these United Colonies*
> *are . . . Free and Independent States . . . And for the*
> *support of this Declaration, with a firm Reliance*
> *on the Protection of divine Providence, we . . . pledge*
> *to each other our Lives, Our Fortunes, and our sacred*
> *Honor.*

On June 28, the convention of Maryland voted for independence. Then word reached Philadelphia that New Jersey was sending new delegates who would vote *yes*.

On July 1, the debate in Congress continued. John Adams rose to his feet.

"Before God, I believe the hour has come," he said. "All that I have, and all that I am, and all that I hope in this life, I am now ready to stake upon it . . . I am for the declaration . . . It is my living sentiment, and . . . my dying sentiment. Independence now, and Independence forever!"

No one spoke. Just then, the door swung open. Dr. John Witherspoon hurried into the room. He and the two other New Jersey delegates were covered with mud.

"Gentlemen," he stated, "New Jersey is ready to vote for independence."

When the vote was taken, eight of the thirteen colonies voted with New Jersey. Pennsylvania and South Carolina voted *no*. New York did not vote. Delaware's two delegates split. Congress set the next day for another vote.

The Patriots knew Delaware was the key. They had to reach Delaware's third delegate, Caesar Rodney. An express rider was dispatched to fetch him.

Rodney was sick with cancer at his home in Dover, Delaware. At two o'clock in the morning, the messenger arrived.

"Sir, you must come to Philadelphia at once," he panted. "The vote is tomorrow."

"Get my horse," Rodney ordered.

The distance to Philadelphia was eighty-nine miles. Rodney galloped furiously. He rode through the cold rains and fierce winds. He crossed muddy rivers and swollen streams. The delegate realized that his vote could make the difference. He also realized that his stand on this issue would destroy any hope he had for curing the cancer. The only doctor who could help him lived in London.

Rodney arrived at one o'clock the next afternoon. Two people carried the exhausted man into the assembly hall.

"Sir, how do you vote?" Chairman John Hancock asked.

"My people favor independence," Rodney declared. "I agree with them. I vote for independence." Rodney slumped into a chair.

Eleven other colonies joined New Jersey and voted in favor of independence. New York did not vote. It was decided.

The thirteen colonies had now become the United States of America.

The afternoon sun shone into the hall. Some of the delegates stared out the tall chamber windows. A few wept. Others bowed their heads, closing their eyes in prayer.

Suddenly, John Hancock broke the silence, "Gentlemen, the price on my head has just doubled!" The men chuckled. Samuel Adams rose to his feet and announced, "We have put God back in His proper place. He reigns in heaven. May His Kingdom come."

The date was July 4, 1776. A new nation had been born. But this nation still had to win its freedom. Would the rays of God's light and glory shine through the battles ahead?

FOURTEEN

*For I consider that the sufferings of this present time
are not worthy to be compared with the glory that is
to be revealed to us. (Romans 8:18)*

THE DARK NIGHT OF A NATION'S SOUL

As news of the Declaration spread, Patriots everywhere celebrated. Church bells rang while guns exploded and crowds cheered. An excited John Adams mailed two letters to his wife Abigail on the same day. In the first, he wrote, "It is the will of heaven that the two countries should be separated forever. It may be the will of heaven that America shall suffer calamities still more dreadful."

In his second letter, Adams predicted that the day the Declaration was passed would be "the most memorable . . . in the history of America." He went on to add, "I am well aware of the toil and blood and treasure that it will cost to maintain this Declaration, and support and defend these States. Yet through all the gloom I can see the rays of ravishing light and glory."

The newborn nation now confronted her greatest challenge. She had to win her independence by resisting the greatest military power on earth. Would she be able to pass the test?

✛ ✛ ✛

The celebration of America's independence quickly died away. As soon as the Redcoats left Boston, Washington transported his troops to New York. He fortified the town of Brooklyn across the East River on the western end of Long Island. The nearby Hudson River was the gateway north. Washington knew the British would want to control it. But that would split the New England colonies in half, and it would help the British crush the rebellion in the north. Washington could not let this happen. He decided to fortify the only obstacle that stood in the way—Brooklyn.

On July 4, the same day the Declaration was passed, British General Howe landed the first of fifty-five thousand men in New York. It was time for battle. By August 18, twenty thousand British troops stood ready on the southeast shore of Brooklyn. Facing them were barely eight thousand Americans under Washington. Five days later, the British had almost surrounded the Americans. Howe ordered an attack on August 27.

Washington watched the action through his field telescope. By afternoon, the Americans were almost trapped. They waited for the final British assault. They waited and waited and waited. Yet, Howe did not attack. Unbelievable!

The next morning, the British still had not moved. All that day, the Americans continued to wait, while the British guns remained silent. In the late afternoon, a cold rain began to fall.

By now, Washington had a plan. "This is giving us valuable time," he told his senior officers. "We might be able to do it."

"Do what, sir?" a brigadier-general asked.

"Move the troops," he replied. "This northeast wind will stop Howe's fleet from entering the East River. We'll ferry our men across by boat and join our forces on Manhattan."

"But sir, it's a full mile across the river!" another general pointed out. "And we have eight thousand troops! Shouldn't we stay and wait for the attack?"

"No," came the reply. Washington had made up his mind.

At first, the Americans battled cold winds and choppy waters. After midnight, the wind died away and the oarsmen guided the small boats through the still waters. Soldiers waited in line to be taken off the beach. Washington stationed a few troops at the front lines so the British would not suspect anything.

And then came dawn. The Patriots still needed three hours to get everyone across. Daylight would give them away. The Americans did not know what to do, but God did. Out of nowhere, a heavy fog began to rise from the ground and water. The American troops could barely see one another. And neither could the British! The Patriots kept on working. The fog remained until Washington and the last boat had left the island. Then it lifted. The British rushed to the shore and started firing, but the Americans were out of range.

It was a miracle. Eight thousand American soldiers had safely escaped before twenty thousand British troops. God's favor was clearly upon the Patriots.

Once again, Howe waited before crossing to Manhattan, just as he had done at Bunker Hill. In the meantime, the Continental Army withdrew from Manhattan and retreated through New Jersey. This pattern of withdrawal before superior forces earned General Washington much respect from his enemy. They began to refer to him as a "cunning fox."

British General Charles Cornwallis, in charge of the New Jersey campaign, pursued Washington until winter. Then he entered winter quarters. But Washington did not. Spirits in the American camp were low. Many of the enlistments would soon be up. The general decided to attack Trenton.

"We'll attack at dawn on December 26," he told his officers. "The German soldiers there won't be expecting anyone the day after Christmas."

As his troops loaded into small boats, a violent snow and hailstorm suddenly came up. Once again, the Continentals had the aid of their strongest Ally. The blinding storm prevented the British guards from detecting a thing. In forty-five minutes of combat, the Americans took a thousand British prisoners.

Cornwallis immediately took troops to Trenton.

"Sir, you must attack at once!" his officers pleaded.

"I can bag the fox in the morning," Cornwallis replied with confidence.

"Sir, if you trust those people tonight," his quartermaster general warned, "you'll see nothing of them in the morning."

The quartermaster was right. In the dead of night, the Continentals stole away, right past Cornwallis's troops. They drove back a support column on its way to join Cornwallis and went on to take Princeton.

Americans everywhere rallied in support of their general and their army. Many new volunteers answered the call to arms.

The general sat on his horse and watched his soldiers shuffle through the falling snow. They were tired and cold. Some had no coats. Others had no boots. The bare feet of a few left bloody footprints in the snow. The general grieved for his men and for his country. They had just lost Philadelphia, the capital of their government, to the British. Liberty and independence seemed like hollow words.

It was December 1778. The soldiers were headed toward Valley Forge, fifteen miles from Philadelphia. Washington had chosen this place as their winter camp.

Snow fell early that winter. The soldiers built cabins, but it was impossible to stay warm. They did not have the proper clothing. Congress had promised to send it but had sent paper money instead. Washington was frustrated. His men were frustrated too.

And they were hungry. Meals consisted of nothing more than "firecake," wheat or cornmeal mixed with water. Sometimes a supply wagon with salt pork or dried fish got through enemy lines. But this was not often. Most of the time, the men remained hungry. By February, they were down to their last twenty-five barrels of flour.

Valley Forge was a time of testing for the American army. In the 1600s Pilgrims and Puritans had faced their starving times. Their grandchildren had suffered the horror of an Indian uprising. Now Valley Forge was the dark night in the young nation's soul. The enemy slept a few miles away in warm quarters. They were eating good food. The Americans were freezing and dying. At Valley Forge, the soldiers had to decide whether to give up their quest for freedom. They had to decide if it was worth the cost.

Their general believed that it was. He knew God would somehow deliver them. But the soldiers had to believe it, too.

God used Valley Forge to forge the iron of the Continental Army into steel.

And He used a special agent to help. Baron von Steuben was a captain from the Prussian army. Washington assigned von Steuben the task of making the men into a professional army.

"No, no!" von Steuben yelled in German, with an English interpreter at his side. "That's not it. You've got to load those muskets together." The men tried again. "That's more like it. I want a crisp volley every fifteen seconds."

"No one is going to desert this army," the captain barked. "You're going to stay and learn how to fight. I'm going to make real soldiers out of you. And you're going to beat those Redcoats!"

Captain von Steuben was a demanding drillmaster. He made the soldiers practice until they got it right. As March turned into April, the soldiers' morale greatly improved. They marched as one. They drilled as one. They could even produce a crisp volley every fifteen seconds.

On the first of May 1778, the American camp received news that France was coming into the war on the side of America. The dark night was over. The French were allies! With that news, volunteers and supplies began pouring in from all over the country. Washington declared a day of thanksgiving.

That spring, General Clinton replaced Howe as commander of the British forces. On June 18, Clinton pulled out of Philadelphia for New York. And the Continental Army swung out of Valley Forge right behind him.

But this was a different army from the one that had trudged down the road six months before. Now there was a sharpness in the beat of the field drums. There was pride in each step. The American Patriots were a real army now.

They caught up with the British at Monmouth. When one of the American field commanders ordered a retreat, Washington spurred to the front of the column. Back and forth he rode, urging the men to form ranks again and giving them an example with his quiet courage. No man could look at him that day and not take heart. The Patriots stopped, turned, and fought the British to a standstill.

Monmouth marked the last time the two main bodies of the British and American armies would be within striking distance. For the next two years, the action involved only small units.

Since the British had not been successful in the north, they looked toward the south. But by 1781, even this southern campaign was not going well. One of the main reasons was the perseverance of the rebel soldiers. As the Patriot Nathanael Greene put it, "We fight, get beat, rise and fight again!" If the Americans could not win by numbers or ammunition, they would win by sheer will power. The tired British army began to make mistakes.

The biggest mistake of all took place at Yorktown, Virginia. Cornwallis was waiting for a British fleet from the north to come for him and his troops. However, a French fleet blocked them from sailing south. Washington now dispatched his combined force of French and American troops to block Cornwallis by land. The British general was surrounded.

On the night of October 16, Cornwallis attempted to ferry his men across the York River. But a sudden, violent storm of wind and rain came up from nowhere. By the time the storm ended, it was too late for the men to move. Cornwallis raised the white flag of surrender the next day.

A gentle breeze stirred the leaves on the sunny afternoon of October 18. In an open field behind Yorktown, the American and French forces formed two lines. The French were dressed in fresh uniforms and new, black-leather leggings. The Americans wore buckskins, homespun shirts, and faded blue-and-white coats known as "continentals".

In the distance came the sound of British marching drums. The officers appeared first on horseback. Then came the soldiers. Some were angry. Some were weeping. The Americans stood straight and tall, watching in silence. "Ground muskets!" each British officer commanded. The soldiers flung their rifles to the ground one by one.

General Cornwallis could not bring himself to turn over his sword in person. He sent a deputy to do it. Washington assigned one of his deputies to accept the sword. When the surrender was finally finished, the American soldiers shouted for joy. The war was over!

The British signed the Treaty of Paris on September 3, 1783. This treaty recognized the independence of the United States. The last British troops left New York in November.

The senior officers of the colonial forces gathered at Fraunce's Tavern in lower Manhattan for the farewell luncheon.

"With a grateful heart," General Washington began, "I now take leave of you." His voice cracked as he tried to hold down his emotions. "Our past days have been filled with glory and honor. I hope your future days will be the same." Washington raised his glass in a toast to his officers.

Then he said, "I would be honored if you would come and take me by the hand."

Henry Knox walked forward. With tears in their eyes, the two men shook hands and embraced each other. One by one, the remaining officers did the same. No one said a word. Nothing needed to be said. These men had fought together and won the independence of their country.

One more duty remained for the General of the Continental Army. He had to resign his commission. He journeyed to Annapolis, Maryland, to appear before Congress.

"Sir, we're prepared to receive your communications," the president of the Congress said.

General Washington rose and bowed to the members. Then he congratulated Congress and the officers who had served him so faithfully. He recalled the names of particular men who had performed courageously in battle.

Washington held his speech with trembling hands.

"As my last official duty, I want to commend the interests of our dear country to the protection of Almighty God," Washington said. "I now take my leave."

Washington pulled his commission from the breast pocket inside his uniform coat and handed it to the president.

At last, he could return home to his beloved Mount Vernon.

CHAPTER

FIFTEEN

Unless the Lord builds the house, They labor in vain who build it. (Psalm 127:1)

BUILDING
THE HOUSE

America was free. Now the nation could obey its special calling from God. This was His plan. From Columbus through the War of Independence, God had been establishing a nation which could live in obedience to His Son, the Lord Jesus. He was creating a fellowship of believers that could become a beacon of light in a world of spiritual darkness. This was a new drama in the history of mankind. God desired this country to demonstrate how He intended for His children to live together under the Lordship of Christ.

But after the war, the United States did not act very united. Individual states feared losing their power and began to act like separate countries. They issued their own currency and taxed other states' goods. Instead of following the Covenant Way, the newborn republic was gradually turning aside.

How would God make sure His plan continued? What would He do to record the Covenant Way for future generations? And what does this mean to us today?

153

✝ ✝ ✝

Many leaders of the new nation saw what was happening and wanted to do something about it. One of these was George Washington, who was home at Mount Vernon.

Washington walked up the long brick path to the main house. A gentle breeze blew in from the Potomac River. He had just finished his early morning ride. As he passed the willows, he thought about how much he loved this place. He was glad to be home now. Yet, his mind could not stop thinking about current events. And a certain sadness filled his heart. *The states are pulling away from the Union,* he thought. *We're not united at all. What did we fight for? What did we die for?*

Washington stepped into his study and sat down at his desk. As he gazed out the window, he prayed, *Lord, help us become one. Help us trust You. Help us live out the Covenant Way of our forefathers.*

Washington pulled a sheet of paper from the drawer. He dipped his quill pen into an ink bottle and began to write another letter. He had begun a letter-writing campaign to the men who were in a position to shape opinion in America.

"Something must be done," he wrote. "The very fabric of our nation is being torn apart. We must work together as a family. If we don't, we'll lose the freedoms we just fought and died for. Something must be done."

The "something" turned out to be a Constitutional Convention in Philadelphia in May 1787. It was held in Independence Hall. After much debate, the delegates decided to write a constitution for the new country. For the first time in history, men had the opportunity to freely write a new constitution for their own government.

The delegates chose George Washington to chair the convention. Washington was God's man for the job. The convention started out as the stormiest one ever held on American soil. But the dignity of Washington's presence preserved the meetings. Washington directed the sessions but never entered the debates. At times, tempers flared as the delegates argued about the issues. But Washington remained neutral. He shared his beliefs only between the sessions. To many Americans, Washington symbolized the spirit of unity.

"We must have a central government that is strong enough to govern our nation," some members argued.

"But the states must keep certain rights," others countered.

"A state's population should determine how many representatives it has," demanded the people from the bigger states.

"No," those from smaller states said. "That would give the larger states power over the smaller states. Each one should have the same number of representatives."

On and on they went, but the debate was deadlocked and growing more bitter. Part of the New York delegation went home in disgust, and others were preparing to leave. But God once again had mercy on the affairs of America. And this time He used the eighty-one-year-old Benjamin Franklin.

The elder statesman rose to his feet. "At the beginning of the war," he said calmly, "we prayed for divine protection. Our prayers were answered.

"I have lived a long time. The longer I live, the more I see that 'God governs in the affairs of man'. A sparrow cannot fall without His notice. Can an empire rise without His aid?"

Franklin wiped his glasses and continued talking. "The Book of Psalms assures us that, 'Unless the Lord builds the house, they labor in vain who build it'. We can build our house in America only with His help.

"I therefore move that from now on, we begin each session in prayer, asking for assistance and blessing from heaven."

This speech marked the turning point. Nearly all of the delegates were Christians of one kind or another. Franklin's words forced them to set their priorities right. The delegates moved forward with the business of crafting a new constitution. They signed it on September 17, 1787.

"We, the people of the United States . . . " These words begin the oldest written constitution still in effect today. It set up a federal system of government which included a national government and separate state governments. It created three branches within the national system: the legislative, executive, and judicial.

The United States Constitution is one of the most astounding documents ever written by man. For two hundred years it has withstood the test of time. Why does it work so well? One reason is that it was divinely inspired. A second is that it was the completion of nearly two hundred years of Puritan political thought. Those early church covenants recognized the sinfulness of man. They anticipated the possibility of human wrong. The Constitution does exactly the same thing. In effect, it documents the Covenant Way on national paper.

On April 30, 1789, George Washington took the oath of office as the first President of the United States. Stepping onto the balcony of Federal Hall in New York, he requested that a Bible be brought. Placing his hand on the Bible, he took the oath of office. A great cheer went up from the crowd as church bells rang and guns exploded.

The new president went inside to deliver his inaugural address to Congress.

"I must express my gratitude to the Almighty," he said. "No people can acknowledge the invisible hand of God more than the people of the United States. Every step toward independence was protected by His hand. Let us remember that the smiles of Heaven will continue on a nation only when it heeds the eternal rules of right and order."

"America, America, God shed His grace on thee . . ."

From the beginning, God has abundantly answered this nineteenth-century prayer we sing so often. There is no way to measure how much of God's grace is poured out on this nation as a result of the obedience of the earliest Christians. But now, the grace seems to be lifting. It is time to heed the warning signs.

The signs are many. They extend from changing weather patterns to violence and drugs. They include incurable diseases and depressed economic times. The list goes on, but it is important only when we realize that it is God's way of getting our attention.

For a whole nation to return to the Covenant Way seems impossible. But it has been done before. We have the biblical example of Nineveh to prove it. Nineveh was the biggest and most powerful city of its age. God was about to destroy it, but He gave it one last chance through the prophet Jonah. Nineveh repented, and the entire city was spared.

Today God is calling Christians everywhere to repent:

And My People,
> who are called by My name,
>> humble themselves
>> and pray,
>> and seek My face
>> and turn from their wicked ways,
> then I will hear from heaven,
>> will forgive their sin,
>> and will heal their land.

2 Chronicles 7:14

We are being called to humble ourselves and walk obediently before the Lord our God.

What does this mean? It means that we must follow Jesus each and every day. It means that we must accept the truth that He is the way, the truth, and the life and that no one comes to the Father but through Him. (John 14:6) It means that we must be willing to be quiet and listen for His still, small voice. It means that we must lay down our own desires and wait for the Holy Spirit to lead us.

Why is this so important? There are two reasons: One is what happens within our own lives, and the second is what happens in the lives of others. God promises blessings to those who follow His ways. These blessings extend to individuals, and they extend to whole countries. A country is only as moral and just as its people.

Today God is calling us to renew our covenant commitment to Him and to one another. If each one of us does this, we will walk in the Light of Christ. Just like a candle, our lives will begin to shine in untold ways. When many of us do this together, we will become His light and His glory . . . for all the world to see.

GLOSSARY

adultery (n) - sexual intercourse outside of marriage

ambush (n) - a surprise attack; (v) to set an ambush

ample (adj) - enough, adequate

artillery (n) - large weapons such as cannons and mounted guns

assault (n) - a sudden attack

banish (v) - to send away or dismiss

batten (v) - to fasten

bilge (n) - stagnant, dirty water

breakers (n) - waves that break into foam

caravel (n) - a fast, small sailing ship

cask (n) - a barrel

charter (n) - a written grant of rights made by a government to a person or a group

commission (n) - an official document in the military which bestows rank

commoner (n) - a person who does not have a title of nobility

compassion (n) - sorrow or pity for others

covenant (n) - a special promise made by two or more persons decompose (v) - to rot or decay

delegate (n) - a representative acting on behalf of a colony or state

drought (n) - a long spell of dry weather, without rain

emigrate (v) - to leave one country to settle in another

enlistment (n) - the period of time for which someone signs up in the military

evangelize (v) - to preach the Gospel

excommunicate (v) - to cut off from the privileges of church membership

executive (adj) - the branch of government which administers the law; (n) the President of the United States is the Chief Executive

fool's gold (n) - pyrite, a metallic ore which looks like gold

fortification (n) - a fortified place

fortify (v) - to strengthen a place against attack

fortress (n) - a fort

friar (n) - a member of a religious order

harbor (n) - a protected section of the sea, used as a port for ships

hatch (n) - an opening in the ship's deck

headwind (n) - a wind blowing against the course of a ship

helmsman (n) - the man who steers a ship

heresy (n) - beliefs outside accepted theology

horizontal (adj) - a position which is parallel to the horizon; the opposite of vertical

hull (n) - the body of a ship

humbly (adv) - to act without pride

immigrant (n) - a person who comes into a new country

inlet (n) - a narrow strip of water between two pieces of
    land
interpreter (n) - a person who translates a foreign language
judicial (adj) - the branch of government which interprets
    the law; judges and courts. The Supreme Court of the
    United States is the highest court in the federal judicial
    branch
legislature (n) - a body of persons with the power to make
    laws for a state or country
maravedis (n) - a Spanish copper coin worth about 1/3 cent
massacre (n) - the killing of a lot of people
merciful (adj) - showing mercy and compassion
monastery (n) - the place in which monks live
morale (n) - the feeling of enthusiasm or courage
musket (n) - a firearm with a long barrel; used by soldiers
    before the rifle was invented
navigation (n) - the plotting of the course of ships
outskirts (n) - the part of a town outside of its center
palisade (n) - a fence of stakes especially for defense
pantaloons (n) - trousers
Parliament (n) - the national legislative body in Britain
patent (n) - title to land
patriot (n) - a person who loves and supports his country
peninsula (n) - land almost entirely surrounded by water
persecute (v) - to treat cruelly over a period of time
perseverance (n) - persistence
provisional (adj) - temporary
redoubt (n) - a fortification
reef (n) - sand or rock that lies near the surface of water
reform (v) - to correct or make better

repent (v) - to be sorry for your sins

repentance (n) - the state of being sorry for your sins

reputation (n) - a person's character in the eyes of others

resent (v) - to take offense

revelation (n) - a disclosure of something

revival (n) - a new interest in religion

revolt (v) - to rebel against the government

ritual (n) - a set form of worship

rudder (n) - a movable piece of wood used for steering a
     boat

scholar (n) - a student

scurvy (n) - a disease caused by the lack of vitamin C; on
     long sea voyages, it was prevented by drinking
     lemon juice

sentry (n) - a guard

shallop (n) - a small open boat, fitted with oars and sails

siege (n) - a military blockade used as an attempt to win
     in battle

starboard (n) - the right-hand side of a ship

steadfast (adj) - sturdy

tactics (n) - military training to oppose an enemy force

tether (v) - to fasten an animal with a rope or chain

tiller (n) - the handle that turns a boat's rudder

tithingman (n) - the man who enforcd the church rules in
     Puritan New England

trespass (v) - to cut across the rights or property of another

'tween-decks (n) - a small area on a ship between two decks

tyrant (n) - a cruel ruler

unanimous (adj) - united in opinion

vertical (adj) - at a right angle to the horizon; the opposite
     of horizontal

volley (n) - firing weapons at the same time, as a group
yoke (n) - something that binds together
zeal (n) - enthusiasm

STUDY QUESTIONS

Chapter 1   **Christ-Bearer**

1.   What reason did Columbus give for sailing into the Atlantic Ocean? Who gave him the idea?

2.   What rewards did Columbus demand from Ferdinand and Isabella? What do these show about his character?

3.   What three miracles happened on the first voyage? Why do you think God waited for Columbus to ask Him for a miracle?

4.   When did Columbus's vision begin to change?   What tempted him to change it?

5.   List three points from this chapter that indicate God did have a plan for America.

Chapter 2   **If Gold Is Your Almighty**

1.   Were King Ferdinand and Queen Isabella Christians? How do you know?

2.   Name two ways God tried to reach Columbus.

3.   Was Columbus a "Christ-bearer" even though he sinned? Why or why not?

Chapter 3   **Martyrs for Jesus**

1. Look up John 12:24. How does this Scripture apply to the first missionaries who came to the New World?

2. Why did God choose monks to spread His Light into the dark land?

3. What did the early monks find when they arrived? What did they do about it?

4. What is a martyr? Name two from this chapter.

5. Compare Father Jogues with Columbus. How were they alike? How were they different?

Chapter 4   **Without God's Blessing**

1. What did the Virginia Company tell people in order to raise money for the new colony? Was this true?

2. What was the real reason the first Jamestown settlers came to the New World?

3. Who was Robert Hunt?

4. Give three reasons God did not bless the colonists at Jamestown.

Chapter 5   **To the Promised Land**

1. What was God's plan for America? How did the Pilgrims fit into it?

2. What happened to the *Speedwell*? Why did God let this happen?

3. Name two events on the *Mayflower* that illustrate God's hand being on the Pilgrims.

4. Why did the Pilgrims write the Mayflower Compact? What did it do?

Chapter 6   **Five Kernels of Corn**

1. What prepared Squanto for his role at Plymouth?

2. Why did the Pilgrims stay at Plymouth when Captain Jones left?

3. Explain the difference in the way the Jamestown settlers and the Pilgrims felt about the following:
   a. planting corn
   b. the Indians
   c. God

4. What were the "five kernels of corn"?

Chapter 7   **Thy Kingdom Come**

1.   Why did the Puritans feel they had to leave England?

2.   What did the Puritans hope to do in the New World?

3.   Who defined covenant love? What did he say?

4.   How did the Pilgrims demonstrate Christian love toward the Puritans?

5.   Did John Winthrop understand the meaning of commitment? Why or why not?

Chapter 8   **The Puritan Way**

1.   What are some adjectives that would describe the Puritans?

2.   The heart of the Puritans' lives was their willingness to deal with what?

3.   God pruned His vineyard in New England for two purposes: to do away with bad growth and to encourage good growth. What three people illustrated this? How?

Chapter 9   **King Philip's War**

1. Why did the Puritans begin to turn their hearts away from God?

2. According to Deuteronomy 8, what do we receive if we obey the commandments of the Lord?

3. What incident touched off the Indian uprising?

4. How did God use the "Praying Indians" to help the colonists?

Chapter 10   **The Great Awakening**

1. The Great Awakening was a revival. Where did it start? What is a revival?

2. Where did George Whitefield begin preaching in the open air as Jesus did?

3. What important message did George Whitefield deliver to the colonists?

4. Where did he preach his last sermon?

THE LIGHT AND THE GLORY FOR CHILDREN

Chapter 11   **"No King but King Jesus!"**

1.   Read 1 Samuel 15:23. What does the Bible say about rebellion?

2.   Is it ever permissible to resist lawful authority? When?

3.   List three tax acts passed by Parliament that hurt the colonists.

4.   How did the other colonies respond when the king closed the port of Boston?

Chapter 12   **War!**

1.   What battle marked the beginning of the War for Independence?

2.   List three instances of God's favor in the battles of Lexington and Concord.

3.   Why do you think General Howe did not pursue Prescott after the Battle of Bunker Hill?

Chapter 13   **The Birth of a Nation**

1.   What were the spiritual secrets of George Washington's leadership? Do you see any of these characteristics in yourself? In others?

2.   Why did the attack on Canada fail?

3.   Give three instances of God's aid to the colonists during the war.

4.   Why was the Declaration of Independence so important?

Chapter 14   **The Dark Night of a Nation's Soul**

1.   How did God help the Americans on Long Island?

2.   What was it like at Valley Forge? What was God's purpose in this?

3.   What European country decided to help the Americans?

4.   Name three British generals who fought in the War.

Chapter 15   **Building the House**

1.   What document sets up the legal framework for God's plan in America?

2.   How did Benjamin Franklin's influence save the Constitutional Convention?

3.   What role can you have in promoting God's plan for our great country?